100 Best Bikes

100 Best Bikes

Zahid Sardar

Laurence King Publishing

Published in 2012 by
Laurence King Publishing Ltd
361–373 City Road
London EC1V 1LR
Tel: +44 20 7841 6900
Fax: +44 20 7841 6910
email: enquiries@laurenceking.com
www.laurenceking.com

A catalog record for this book is available from the
British Library.

ISBN 13: 978 1 7806 700 89

Design: Intercity
www.intercitystudio.com

Printed in China

Contents

Introduction
The Safety Bike
Zahid Sardar

Recently, some friends and I took sturdy red Batavus MacBikes out north of central Amsterdam into a landscape of out-of-the-way dikes, medieval streets, and secret gardens. The thrill of pedaling from a bustling city to a country adventure only a few miles away is still palpable and I realize that this is why, unlike other nineteenth-century inventions that have long disappeared, the bike is here to stay. It spells freedom.

One hundred examples of bikes by both well-known manufacturers and unknown individuals from around the globe that are included here epitomize the widespread twenty-first-century bicycle renaissance. The modern bike's enviable agility and versatility have even prompted car manufacturers and aerospace designers to craft new versions of this remarkable invention. Relatively recently, Porsche, Ferrari, BMW, Mercedes Benz, and Audi have engineered lighter, aerodynamic bikes with hollow monocoque frames made of carbon fiber, aluminum, titanium, plywood, and the kind of bamboo used for Asian rickshaws. Sealed gear hubs, disc brakes, LED lights, and solar-powered batteries are other sophisticated improvements and yet, in essence, bikes are nothing more than frames, wheels, handlebars, cranks, pedals, gears, brakes, and saddles.

What is remarkable is that the first French and British iterations of this simple two-wheeled 1860s wonder – clownish and hard to ride Penny-farthing or high-wheeler bikes – became nearly obsolete by the turn of the century. The iconic safety bike that emerged in their stead remained unchallenged for decades until the rising twentieth-century preference for cars, especially in North America.

The safety bike, on which most modern bikes are modeled, survived even this threat because of its smaller twin wheels, simple easy-to-weld diamond-shape frame of tubular steel and high handlebars that allowed upright sitting and better maneuverability. With a lower center of gravity the safety bike was not unwieldy; it could go fast, be mounted and dismounted effortlessly, and brought to a halt at will. Riding it was faster than walking and it cost far less to run than a horse or car.

Incremental refinements changed the safety bike only slightly until the 1970s when suddenly, thanks to a few renegade tinkerers in California, the bike changed in form and its use expanded beyond short-distance commuting or racing.

Teenagers in East Los Angeles who coveted unaffordable low-riding dragster cars began to modify bikes so that they resembled cars and motorbikes. Inspired by these new geometries, American bike manufacturer Schwinn introduced Al Fritz's Sting-Ray cruiser in 1963. Californian John West and his son Angus transformed one of these into Spawn, an influential custom low-rider with extravagant, garish styling, and hundreds of others followed suit.

Two decades later in the San Francisco Bay Area, Joe Breeze, who is considered the father of modern mountain bikes, hand-built rugged frames for off-road mountain trails. Copycat bikes emerged with unusual aluminum frames, enhanced suspension, and maneuverability that allowed fearless riders to climb, soar, or summersault ever higher. Extreme sports bikes were born.

Although safety bikes continued to be indispensable modes of transportation in parts of Europe, Japan, China, India, and Africa after the Second World War, in North America the car might have nudged the bike into oblivion had it not been for the innovations of these young daredevils.

Although mountain bikes originated in California, British engineer Alex Moulton pioneered the use of conical rubber springs and small wheels for improved suspension in the British Motor Corporation's 1950s Mini car. He replicated that idea for his 1962 small-wheeled, easy-to-dismantle Moulton bike that was not just comfortable to ride but swift enough to win some of bike racing's greatest trophies. Moulton's pioneering concepts undoubtedly inspired other British designers such as Andrew Ritchie, who created the modular folding Brompton in 1979, and Mark Sanders, who designed the portable folder

Opposite
Union Station bike shelter

Right (from top)
Batavus bikes, Amsterdam
Joseph Bellomo's arc shelter

STRiDA in 1987, as well as southern California designer David Hon, a former laser physicist who founded Dahon in 1982 and mass manufactured his folding bike designs in Asia.

The United States, still a leader in handmade bikes from virtually every urban center in the country, is poised to take advantage of a trend all across Europe, Japan, and parts of Asia that again favors the bike as the best kind of urban transportation. With a greater interest in reducing carbon emissions and traffic jams in cities, more and more people are opting for bikes and mass transit. They are riding to work, to school, and to the supermarket. The ubiquitous black granny and grandpa Batavus bikes have been repackaged as the bright red, sturdily built, theftproof MacBikes we rented outside Amsterdam's central railway station. Cities are re-zoning streets as bike lanes and some metropolises like Paris, Barcelona, London, and Montreal have unleashed thousands of share bikes that anyone can borrow. Following their lead, New York has commissioned 40,000 Alta Bicycle Share bikes from Portland, Oregon, and the Dutch team West 8 (founded by landscape architect Adriaan Geuze) will design a 40-acre park for Governors Island replete with 3,000 wooden bicycles for visitors.

Lighter bikes boosted with battery power will help riders climb even the steep hills of San Francisco. Designers are confidently rethinking the bike and even devising sophisticated storage shelters for it.

Bikestation, a Long Beach, California business launched in 1996, was modeled after Japanese and European examples, and is the first full-service membership storage and repair facility for bicyclists next to a metro station in the United States. The enterprise has expanded to other cities. In Palo Alto, California, architect Joseph Bellomo has created modular acrylic and aluminum bike arc shelters that can be used on sidewalks, at bus stations, and train stations. Perhaps the most arresting and iconic reminder of this growing bike movement is Washington, DC's magnificent steel and glass bike shelter for 150 bikes in front of historic Union Station. The hump-shaped structure with operable fins of fretted glass for natural ventilation and controlling heat gain, was designed by KGP architects.

For designers, and even former track racing champions intent on maximizing bike use, no idea is too absurd. New York architecture firm Manifesto has a Ferris wheel-style concept for storing bikes vertically against skyscrapers in crowded cities like Seoul. Dutch designers Merel Sloother, Liat Azulay, and Pieter Frank de Jong have created a cruiser that plays musical records on its wheels. At ECAL, an industrial design school in Lausanne, Switzerland, Christophe Machet has

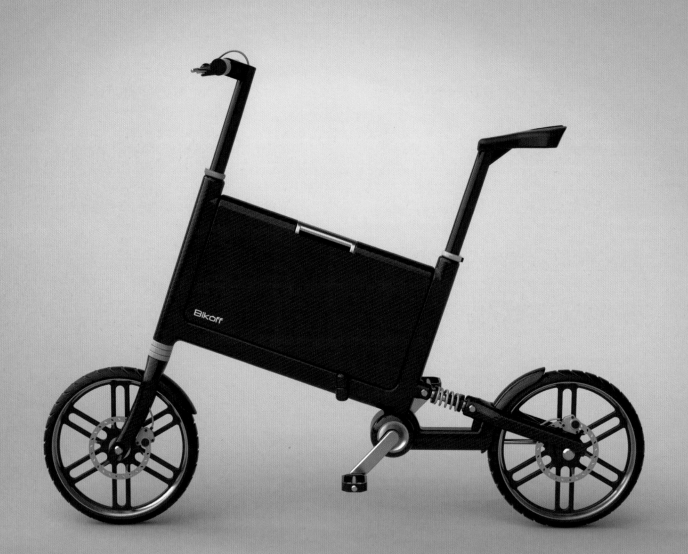

Opposite
Marcos Madia's Bikoff

Right (from top)
Christophe Machet's Camioncyclette
Dario Pegorett'si Zahid
Why Not? Pegoretti bike frame

fashioned Camioncyclette, a large shopping basket on wheels complete with pedals. Bikoff by Marcos Madia in Argentina, is a folding bike that includes a snappy briefcase that locks into the frame. British Olympics gold medalist Chris Boardman now also promotes his eponymous brand of sporty urban bikes. Viennese product designer Valentin Vodev who has the distinction of being the only trike designer included here explains how he has improved three wheels: "It behaves like a bike. Trikes, like buses, lumber ahead in a straight line, but my electric trike turns and curves exactly like a bike."

Australian furniture designer Gary Galego suggests that the bike is like a piece of furniture that moves. Other bike designers speak of comfort on a bike as if it were a chair and, not surprisingly, several of the bike designers included in this book are also furniture and product designers: Marc Newson of Australia, Hong Kong's Michael Young, Tjeerd Veenhooven from Holland, Ross Lovegrove from England, and Joey Ruiter from the United States.

For flat Denmark, MIT researchers have created the Copenhagen Wheel, a battery-powered rear wheel that offers boosts and extends riding distances. In Copenhagen, Biomega founder Jens Martin Skibsted's colorful, creative hybrid bikes make the same bike equally practical for riding in cities and on mountain trails. Skibsted also designs

bikes for German sportswear company Puma as well as with KiBiSi, his multifarious design partnership with Lars Larsen and Bjarke Ingels Group (BIG).

BIG, a firm that believes the best design solutions for future cities include bikes, sometimes creates buildings in the shape of mountains and in the case of Building 8, a ten-story residential complex in suburban Copenhagen, bicyclists can actually ride up to their front doors.

BIG amplified its concept of integrating buildings and bicycle paths during the Shanghai Expo 2010. The firm's Danish Pavilion building was essentially a spiraling ramp around a pool of water with Copenhagen's original Little Mermaid in the middle. Visitors could cycle all the way to the top on one of a thousand free share bikes.

Architect Bjarke Ingels and other designers who question existing urban paradigms may inevitably alter the safety bike too. "Why Not?" is the response of maverick Italian designer Dario Pegoretti whose unorthodox, expressionistic painted bike frames have challenged conventional bike graphics for decades.

Some international designers riff on urban bikes

Alex Moulton

"Design nowadays is all styling," says Alex Moulton, the upper-crust inventor of rubber suspension for the small-wheeled Mini car. He famously applied similar suspension principles to his F-frame bike, the Moulton.

"I was the pioneer of the small-wheel suspension bike that is nice to ride," he says.

Moulton's design fared really well in Japan because "the Japanese are extremely open to innovation and they appreciate good functional design," he says. "My design has a geometry that keeps the bike horizontal rather than driving down. This is a very nice feeling. The Moulton is for riding."

The Brompton folding bike, the portable STRiDA bike, and even the full-suspension mountain bike owe much to Moulton. "I feel very flattered that people do recognize that the Moulton was the original thing in 1962," he says.

Bjarke Ingels

"Cities are becoming myopic in their interest in cars," says Danish architect Bjarke Ingels, the founding principal of BIG architects who commutes between Copenhagen and New York. "It is better to have vehicles that are most efficient. It is not that the bicycle is a new paradigm but for urban mobility the bicycle is the most efficient."

In a community of townhouses with gardens that BIG designed in Copenhagen, bike ramps lead to front doors on all floors.

"Still, I doubt that such bike buildings will be the norm. You can eliminate parking to encourage public transportation, but you need to make the most efficient movement available," Ingels says. "In New York I have a Puma folding bicycle to go to work and a car to go out of the city."

Chris Boardman

"I love to see bikes becoming more popular as forms of transport rather than seeing them used only in races," says British Olympic medalist Chris Boardman, who has a brand of bikes that carry his name.

His urban bikes are as exciting as any racing bike, he suggests. "We build some elegance into every design, because beauty and function are synonymous. Function is by far the most beautiful thing, and the machine that does everything it needs to without fuss tends to look more beautiful," he says.

Boardman's racing experience also has a big effect on his bike designs. "We don't make super-light bikes that flex or TT bikes that are super aerodynamic but don't handle properly, forcing the rider out of their aerodynamic tuck all the time."

Craig Calfee

Craig Calfee, a pioneering carbon fiber frame builder from San Francisco, California, now works in Santa Cruz and produces Bamboosero, an affordable bamboo bike manufactured in Uganda.

The original Calfee Bamboo bike started as a trade show gimmick in 1995. "I had heard that bamboo bikes were built in the 1890s with metal lugs, but I wanted to develop a frame with any tubular material that could be bound together with carbon fiber."

Bamboo was strong; it was shock absorbent and green.

"Bamboo can also be heated and bent if needed," Calfee says.

To make the frame he used epoxy reinforced with carbon fibers around mitered bamboo joints. When the carbon fiber joints proved too inert for natural bamboo that tends to breathe, he switched to Chinese hemp fiber. "It's like Asian scaffolding."

Gary Galego

Australian furniture designer Gary Galego, whose work has been praised even in Milan, designed Carbonwood, a laminated wood and carbon fiber bike for a 2009 show in Sydney called Workshopped. His "mobile piece of furniture aims to show what is possible with wood," Galego says.

The bike's award-winning mold-formed laminated wood- and-carbon fiber frame is meticulously crafted like furniture and showcases the merits of innovatively conjoined wood and carbon fiber. For its volume, the composite frame is extremely light and far stronger than solid wood. "The wood layers are an aesthetic decision and not an environmental one. A bike like this cannot be recycled but it will gain a patina," Galego says. "Objects that get used, maintained and repaired, and are then passed on to others rather than thrown away are green."

Graham Hill
Graham Hill, the founder of Treehugger.com, became the designer of German company Schindelhauer's ThinBike when he sought a full-sized alternative to his portable folding STRiDA 5 bike that could also be stored in the narrow hallway of his New York City apartment.

"I like bikes that take up very little space and are also easier to take on the subway," he said. "I wanted to create a really thin, full-size bike that was not awkward to handle and store. Usually, the chains are greasy and the handlebars and pedals are too wide."

Schindelhauer makes bikes with a greaseless carbon belt drive on a frame that has a rear triangle that can be opened on the chain side. Hill asked them to add MKS folding pedals and a Speedlifter Twist handlebar. "I had been sketching handlebar solutions but this

was a great pre-existing one that Schindelhauer recommended," Hill said. "I took it."

Jens Martin Skibsted
Copenhagen designer and entrepreneur Jens Martin Skibsted had bikes customized for himself as a young man and in time concluded that appealing, colorful hybrid bikes like his could help to reduce the number of cars in cities.

He founded Skibsted Ideation, a branding company and Biomega Bicycles, and later co-founded KiBiSi, a multi-pronged design studio to focus on more innovation. His goal was to design easier-to-maintain and hard-to-steal urban bikes that could be used just as easily to transport kids or groceries.

Skibsted says, "Better-looking bikes that also help us do simple daily tasks in cities will also help us environmentally."

To create new geometries for urban bikes he observed favorites like the Long John, Schwinn Sting-Ray, STRiDA, Moulton AM Speed, Raleigh Type Roadster, Pinarello, and Chinese Little Blue Hat delivery bikes – to name a few.

"Manufacturers apply a sports paradigm for all bikes," Skibsted says. "The future bike has to be less complex and more multipurpose. It has to be sturdy, not light. It needs to be expressive, integrated, and simple to use."

Tokyo, a recyclable aluminum frame bike with one-piece molded forks and mudguards

of carbon fiber, will join his now large series of urban bikes that comes closer to being all those things. He still has on his wish list "an integrated GPS tracking and a remote-controlled locking system."

Joey Ruiter

Aerospace and furniture designer Joey Ruiter designed an all black, aggressively pared down inner-city bike in Grand Rapids, USA, as part of an art competition and has now decided to actually produce it. "I felt that most urban bikes are overdone and over-wrought," Ruiter said. His goal: to reduce the bike to two wheels, a mechanism to move it forward, a seat, and grips. "The rest is all excess," he says.

"It was fun to create a new icon that goes back to the 'first' bike. It is like the Model T car and has just the right mix of ergonomics, comfort, and simplicity."

The finished bike, composed of pre-manufactured parts that are assembled and not welded together, will have a carbon drive and will require almost no maintenance. "It will only have a couple of bolts."

"It is a new kind of city bike that is part beach cruiser with thick 36-inch wheels for speed and a short wheel base," Ruiter says. "That's great if you want to ride a mile or two, but anything beyond that is too much. It's like wearing high heels to dinner. You can't jog in them."

Mark Sanders

On most days, British designer Mark Sanders, a former Royal College of Art student who now teaches there when he is not busy designing kitchen devices for the elderly, is seen riding the foldable STRiDA bike he designed in 1987.

"Actually I did a long apprenticeship with Rolls Royce and I went to a big engineering college and my background was all engineering. It was inhuman and about machinery. I was into stuff that people could relate to and so I went back to RCA and studied human-centered design. That was nirvana."

His long, 22-mile commute into central London, prompted Sanders to think of designing a portable bike that could be brought into a train compartment – but his teacher tried to dissuade him: "The bike has been done. Go on to something else."

However, believing that a triangular frame of lightweight aluminum tubing, coupled with a belt drive and folding mechanisms was possible, Sanders persevered. "That aim of linking transport and going on a bike to the end of the journey was the real target of my project. I was doing the very journey every day," Sanders said.

"It is frowned upon to design for yourself but now I say to my students that if you can include yourself in the problem you will have a stronger incentive for it to work."

Michael Young

"I used to bicycle but I had one too many misses in Hong Kong," says British industrial designer Michael Young, who spends his time between studios in Brussels and Hong Kong. "Cycling is not very respected in Hong Kong."

Still, Young, who designs interiors and furniture, has also created sleek urban bikes for Taiwan-based Giant, the world's largest producer of bicycles.

At Giant's Taichung factory Young learned about hydroforming to reshape aluminum tubing without cutting it. The first bike Young designed was a neutral aluminum bike with nice details, but the second one is sleeker with integrated lights, a concealed locking cable, and modern details within the frame, all made possible by what he learned about water shaping. "It was like a marriage. I went to the factory once a month for almost three years," he said.

Ross Lovegrove

Ross Lovegrove, whose nature-inspired forms for chairs and lighting often resemble spaceships, rides a bike to work. He doesn't think that bikes are like moving furniture, nor should they be. "The physiodynamics of a chair are completely different and frankly who would want to sit on a hard slim saddle all day?" he asks. However, when designing either a chair or a bike, "the trinity of material, technology, and form are always important."

Opposite
STRiDa 5

His London (LDN) bike for Biomega has a one-piece, utilitarian molded carbon fiber form "that is dynamic and unisex," Lovegrove says. His Rio bamboo bike has aluminum lug joints that allow the natural tubing to be replaced by lighter carbon fiber tubes when required. His newest SKIN concept bike will have a monocoque frame with a surface designed for solar gain.

Sjoerd Smit
Dutch entrepreneurs Taco and Ties Carlier launched Van Moof bikes in Amsterdam with the help of Red Dot award-winning industrial designer Sjoerd Smit.

"We looked at the bike. We wanted to make this elegant machine simpler, theftproof, and more pleasurable for the urban dweller," Smit said. "We wanted to make it more functional, good-looking, and affordable."

With such bikes on the road, he hopes that more cities around the globe will opt for them and not the car.

"In too many places bikes are still mainly for leisure or exercise," Smit says.

Smit's thick sturdy tubular aluminum Van Moof frame is for riding Dutch-style everyday, anywhere, and at any time. "We worked on integrating the light, fenders, brakes, and lock in the frame for safety. We included all the essentials," he says.

Søren Sögreni
Three decades ago, Copenhagen designer Søren Sögreni sought to improve bikes he considered boring.

He started by rescuing abandoned bikes and raiding their parts for inspiration. "I learned from old bike mechanisms, the Lotus Seven I drive, from furniture, and from classical Japanese design," he said. "Inspiration came from many sources. I changed bikes by improving a lot of small details. Better lights, better bells, better mudguards."

A silver alloy Sogreni bike with a sterling silver bell and other refinements is permanently displayed at the Georg Jensen silver showroom in Copenhagen. Sögreni's famous shop in a small side street in Copenhagen also draws tony customers who snap up the hundred odd, relatively expensive, museum-worthy city bikes he crafts each year.

"My bikes are like Fritz Hansen furniture. They are well made, basic, and do not try to respond to the latest fashion."

Pricing key:

Under $1,000:	⚲
Under $2,000:	⚲⚲
Under $5,000:	⚲⚲⚲
Under $10,000:	⚲⚲⚲⚲
Over $10,000:	⚲⚲⚲⚲⚲

*All weights given for the bikes in the following pages are approximate because of variable components.

Race
/Tour

Focus
2011 Izalco Chrono 1.0 Road Bike

16–18 lb (7.25–8.16 kg)
$$$$
focus-bikes.com

Derby, a European corporation, produces Focus bikes in Germany. Initiated in 1992 by cyclocross champion Mike Kluge, Focus only makes sports and urban bikes designed by pros and athletes. Kluge's own victories on Focus mountain bikes attracted production with Derby Cycle Werke, the sponsorship of the first German professional mountain bike team and Team Milram, and a presence at the 1996 Olympics in Atlanta. Jörg Arenz, who became a German cyclocross champion on a Focus bike, is now a Focus brand manager.

The first Focus carbon frames in 2006 led to one of the most aerodynamic series of time-trial bikes in the world: the Izalco Chrono 1.0, developed with time-trial expert Andreas Walser. Fitted with the top-brand groupset, SRAM Red, it garnered international wins for Focus athletes. Its strengths, including tapered tubes to reduce weight and wind-resistance, are now featured even in less expensive Focus bikes, according to design engineer Fabian Jaekel. The powder-coated 20-gear Izalco Chrono has a tapered head tube, carbon dropouts, a carbon layup, a reinforced integrated cable tunnel that enhances stiffness, 3T Aura-Pro Aero Carbon OS handlebars, a Focus Carbon time-trial seatpost, a Prologo Nago Tri 40 saddle, and 28-in Zipp 808 wheels.

Focus
2011 Izalco Chrono 1.0
Road Bike

Kestrel
4000 Pro SL Ultegra

20 lb (9.07 kg)
$$$$
kestrelbicycles.com

Nearly three decades of design and engineering expertise in producing molded carbon-fiber bikes means that Kestrel, which pioneered its work in Santa Cruz and is now based in Philadelphia, produces tri racing bikes that are stiff, strong, lightweight, ride well, are comfortable, and are guaranteed to last. The blue and white Kestrel 4000 Pro SL Ultegra for triathletes, a design revived from Kestrel's archives but with frame improvements, is in many ways like other double-diamond carbon-fiber frames with seat tubes. However, like other Kestrels, it has hidden strengths: a modular monocoque structure, longer fibers that run from one tube through a junction into another tube, aerospace-grade adhesives, hollow, bladder-molded stay assemblies that

add strength and beauty to the frame, and CNC tooling for precise functional aerodynamics.

Oval Composites, Kestrel's component house brand, features prominently in the 4000 series, which has low Oval Concepts W745 650c wheels with Vittoria Rubino Pro Foldable tires, an Oval ST700 Tri saddle with titanium rails, a Kestrel Aero Carbon seatpost, several group options from Ultegra to SRAM Red and Shimano Di2, Ultegra chain and cassette, Tektro brake calipers, and A900 brake levers with the pricey Oval Concepts aerobar.

Kestrel
4000 Pro SL Ultegra

Porsche
Bike RS

20 lb (9.07 kg)
$$$$
porsche-bike.com

Some years ago, Porsche introduced an extraordinary yellow and black Porsche FS Evolution mountain bike that echoed its car brand. In 2011, Porsche Design Driver's Selection introduced two new hybrid road bikes, one made of carbon fiber and the other of aluminum. Both have a similar design heft replete with current construction and technological innovations. The Porsche Bike RS (Rennsport or motor racing) monocoque carbon frame is designed for racing and touring, but can be adapted for city use. The top tube, wishbone seatstays, and integrated head tube are combined in one sweeping arc like a cantilevered step-through that makes the bike easier to mount or dismount. Each frame also has a code number that can be registered at a website that helps to track stolen bikes that come up for sale.

With the expected lightness, stiffness, and damping properties of carbon fiber, the RS sports 20-speed Shimano XTR gears, a Crank Brothers Cobalt 11 mountain bike stem and flat handlebars, a Fi'zi:k Tundra 2 K:ium rail saddle, Crank Brothers Candy 3 pedals, 29-in Crank Brothers wheels with puncture-resistant Schwalbe Marathon Supreme tires, hydraulic Magura MT8 disc brakes, and carbon brake levers.

Porsche
Bike RS

Colnago
CX-1 Road Bike

15 lb (6.8 kg)
$$$
colnago.com

Racing enthusiast Ernesto Colnago launched his bike brand in 1954, and the company went on to produce classics such as the Master, the much-lauded C50, the EPS, and many other worthy racing bicycles. Shorter, more upright, frames were Colnago's contribution to modern racing bicycle geometry. Other innovations included a custom titanium stem welded in the United States to aid champion Eddy Merckx's assault on the hour record. When carbon-fiber composite materials became available, Colnago was the first to embrace them. Collaborations with Ferrari Engineering and the Politecnico di Milano helped produce Colnago's Concept and C35, the precursors of most carbon and CX-1 frames. A one-piece monocoque front triangle built with new lamination technology and an alfa-carbon blend, as well as computer-designed polygonal cross-section tubes, add rigidity for sprints and uphill cycling. Bonded seatstays and chainstays dampen bumps for a more comfortable ride.

Colnago
CX-1 Road Bike

NeilPryde
Diablo Alpine Road Bike

15 lb (6.8 kg)
$$$–$$$$
neilprydebikes.com

BMW Group's subsidiary DesignworksUSA typically sculpts train, yacht, and car forms, but now its Singapore branch has shaped a set of high-performance carbon-fiber bike frames for Hong Kong–based NeilPryde, the windsurfing and water sports equipment manufacturer. Wind-tunnel testing of several shapes led to NeilPryde's aerodynamic Alize and Diablo frames. The Diablo, intended for alpine racing enthusiasts who want an extra boost from a lighter, tougher bike, has a lightweight carbon-fiber monocoque structure that is faceted and ribbed strategically along the tapered top bar and down tubes – not unlike some surfboards – for strength and to reduce frame weight. Fork blades, chainstays, and seatstays were all reinforced with stiffness ribs and all frame joints are slightly swelled like butted metal conjunctions.

Diablo, a winner of the IF, Red Dot, and Good Design Awards, comes with a Selle Italia saddle, Shimano Dura-Ace 7900 or Shimano Ultegra and FSA SLK components, and a 2011 Ksyrium SF wheelset from Mavic and Hutchinson with Atom Comp tires.

NeilPryde
Diablo Alpine Road Bike

Boardman Bikes
Elite series AiRTT9.8

16 lb (7.25 kg)
$$$$$
boardmanbikes.com

The AiR (Aerodynamic Racing) TT frames, designed by legendary British bicycling medalist Chris Boardman, are more than notable. Boardman won gold at the Olympics, the World Championships, and the Commonwealth Games; now, from his eponymous company, Boardman Bikes, he leads the research and development of every category of bike in the company's repertoire.

Other champions have won titles on these high-performing bikes because of Boardman's expertise, but the bikes win on looks, too. The Elite and Pro series in every category have an elegance beyond the logistics of performance, as seen in this AiRTT9.8. The bike's features include an ultralight aerodynamic UD (unidirectional) carbon-fiber monocoque frame and tapered steerer, internal cable routing, AiR/TT aerodynamic ultralight UD full carbon fork and integrated brake, SRAM Red gears, Zipp R2C shifters, SRAM Red brakes, Vision Carbon TT chainset, Zipp Sub 9 disc rear wheel, and Zipp 1080 or Zipp 404 front wheel. The broad down tube and seat tube, notched at the bottom to accommodate the back wheel, are wind-tunnel-developed and aerodynamically tuned within the shortened, precise racing geometry.

Boardman Bikes
Elite series AiRTT9.8

Crescent
Hamra 307, 27-VXL

29 lb (13.15 kg)
$$
crescent.se

Crescent, a bike company that originated in the United States during the 1890s, has since the 1960s become quintessentially Swedish and is currently one of Cycleurope's many brands. The bikes were originally imported from the United States and sold in Stockholm. Crescent and its sister brand Monark became the dominant brands in Swedish and Scandinavian racing. Swedish champions Erik and Sture Pettersson won several world titles from 1967 to 1969 on orange Crescents, and their other brothers Gösta and Tomas rode Monarks to victory, adding to their reputation and securing their place in racing lore.

The most recent hybrid Crescent road bikes, like the black and orange Hamra 307, sport the classic racing profile with a sloped top bar, aluminum triple-reduced welded tubular frames, and flat aluminum handlebars. The Hamra comes in a range of frame sizes, all with integrated cabling, a Suntour NCX-D RL front fork, Shimano gear drive, reflective Kenda tires, Shimano hydraulic disc brakes, a Shimano Alivio derailleur, a Spectra saddle on a black alloy seatpost, Spectra wheels, Shimano cranks, a rotating chain case, Spectra chain, and Shimano sprockets.

Seven
Kameha SLX

10 lb (4.5 kg)
$$$$$
sevencycles.com

Since 1997, Seven Cycles founder Rob Vandermark and his team in Massachusetts have been making custom high-modulus carbon-fiber, filament-wound carbon-fiber, custom-butted, and straight-gauge seamless titanium bike frames, as well as steel road, track, mountain, and tandem frames. Reaming, chasing, machining, welding, molding, finishing, and painting are all carried out under one roof. A custom titanium stem and mountain bike handlebar, a carbon-fiber road fork, as well as aluminum handlebars, stems, and seatposts made on site grace off-the-shelf or custom Seven bikes. Seven selects the right tube diameter and wall thickness to suit a rider's weight, age, and riding terrain, and builds every frame to order. The

Kameha SLX, a high-modulus carbon-fiber triathlon bike that is stiff, aerodynamic, and has a slightly sloped top tube and a striking orange and white profile, is among Seven's most expensive bikes. It can be kitted out with SRAM Red, Shimano Di2, or Campagnolo Super Record gearsets, as well as other less expensive gearsets. Zipp Zedtech wheels with Tufo Elite Pulse tires and SRAM Red cranks are other options.

Surly
Long Haul Trucker

32 lb (14.51 kg)
$$
surlybikes.com

The Surly Long Haul Trucker, or Surly LHT, is built for riding longer distances and for carrying things. From Minnesota, Surly's sleek 4130 chromoly (high-carbon) steel long-haul trucker touring bike is versatile with its low bottom bracket, long chainstays, and mounts for fenders and racks. The triangulated double-butted TIG-welded thick-walled wide-diameter frame tubing makes the bike stable even when weighted with cargo. All these Surly frames, with 4130 chromoly lugged and brazed forks, support a popular 26-in wheel size, making replacement tubes, tires, and rims easy to find. Smaller wheels are also stronger than their bigger 700c counterparts for comfortable load-carrying on rough roads. Mud and fender clearances are sufficient for big tires if desired. Tektro Oryx cantilever or linear-pull brakes, Shimano derailleurs and bar-end 9-speed shift levers, silver aluminum handlebars with black Co-Union cork mix webbing, and extra DT Swiss stainless-steel spokes are possible builds. Pedals are not included.

Bianchi
Oltre Super Record

8–12 lb (3.62–5.44 kg)
$$$$$
bianchi.com

Edoardo Bianchi, who won an international Grand Prix of Paris (a prelude to the Tour de France), founded the legendary Milanese company Bianchi in 1885. His company, now under Cycleurope, is a global brand.

While the company has yielded to the vogue for affordable city bikes, it continues its racing philosophy and its search for leaner, meaner machines. The high-end Oltre (oltre is Italian for "beyond") Campagnolo Super Record has a computer-generated carbon frame that is lightweight, rigid, and aerodynamic; its so-called X-Tex design features mold-formed criss-crossed ribbing within the head tube area to add strength and impact-resistance to a hollow form. A secret process also allows Bianchi to mold thinner layers

of tough carbon fiber without wrinkling. A bowed top tube, a fat faceted down tube, and a thick bottom bracket junction give the frame its fierce look, contrasted by very slender seatstays and an almost wedge-shaped seat tube that is tapered at the bottom. The thick bottom bracket contains internal bearings and also adds stiffness. A Fi'zi:k Antares rail braided carbon saddle, 11-speed Campagnolo derailleurs, cranksets, chains, sprockets, brakes and shifters, Fulcrum racing speed XLR carbon tubular wheels, and Vittoria Diamante Pro Light tires are among the features. The Oltre's signature Celeste blue and white color echoes the Bianchi flag.

Orbea
Ordu S105

15 lb (6.8 kg)
$$$
orbea.com

Based in the Spanish Pyrennees, Orbea, a former arms manufacturer, in 1930 began making bikes that today are among the world's best. Among the wide Orbea range made of aluminum and carbon fiber, bikes such as the Ordu GDR carry professional Tour de France teams to Grand Tour mountain-stage wins and others to Olympic competition.

Also fine-tuned for an aerodynamic advantage, this Ordu S105 time trial/triathlon bicycle has a high-modulus carbon-fiber, guaranteed-for-life monocoque frame that is super-light but has exceptional stiffness, built for powerful, bullet-speed amateur riders.

Wind-tunnel-testing in San Diego, California, helped to sculpt the thinner head tube, seat mast, twin-position seatpost, bottom bracket shell, integrated seat clamp, and aero dropouts. The handpainted frame with internal cable guides can be paired with Shimano 105 brakesets and cranks, Orbea Triathlon or Mavic Cosmic Elite wheels with Vittoria Rubino Pro 700x23 tires, an Orbea Ordu Carbon 74/76 seatpost, and a Selle Italia SL T1 saddle.

Orbea
Ordu S105

Van Nicholas
Pioneer Rohloff

20 lb (9.07 kg)
$$$
vannicholas.com

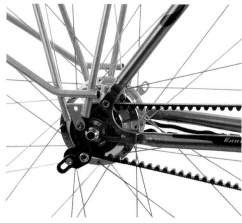

Heavy-duty aerospace-grade titanium is more affordable now, and it rules at Van Nicholas, the Dutch bike frame-building firm offering complete custom-built hand-brushed chemically engraved titanium bikes online. Founded in 1999 by Jan-Willem Sintnicolaas, the firm favors the material's intrinsic beauty, strength, weight, non-corrosive, and easy-to-repair qualities. It guarantees the frames for life.

Van Nicholas' Pioneer Rohloff, intended for commuting and touring, is simple and fail-proof. It has no hydraulic cables, no derailleurs, and no front suspension. A slightly curved titanium seatpost and tough Schwalbe Big Apple balloon tires add comfort, while its integrated 14-gear Rohloff system (like having 27 MTB gears) for one-handed shifting while stationary or pedaling is easy to use. The oversized chainstays are tapered and ovalized, and the traditional round-shaped top, down, and seat tubes are complemented by hourglass-tapered seatstays. Its optional belt drive is lighter, cleaner, and quieter than a regular chain.

Reliable in the most demanding terrain, Pioneer is also a workhorse capable of carrying heavy loads on its seatstay and dropout rack mounts. Designed to take V-brakes or cantilever brakes, it has an English-threaded bottom bracket and traditional headset. A CNC-sculpted chainstay bridge and titanium dropouts, an extended seat tube that increases the standover height, fender mounts, and welded water bottle bosses are other features.

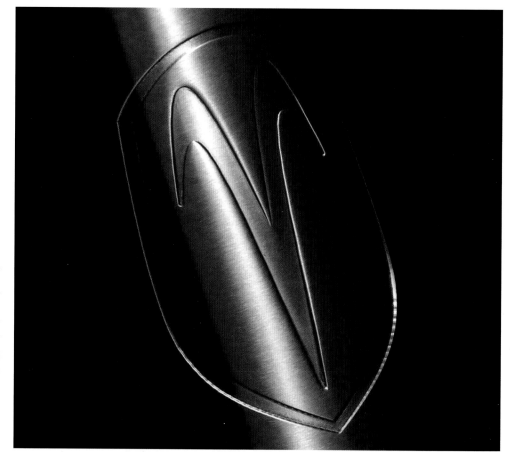

Van Nicholas
Pioneer Rohloff

Stevens
Ridge Max

28 lb (12.7 kg)
$$$
stevensbikes.de

Few companies win as many design awards and racing championships as Stevens, based in Hamburg, Germany. A wholesaler of premium components such as Merlin Titanium, Ritchey, Shimano, and Campagnolo, Stevens began to produce mountain and trekking bikes as well as carbon race and mountain bike frames during the 1990s. Police squads in Hamburg and Canada rode Stevens bikes for their fine suspension, and pro-riders Andreas Kappes and Sascha Henrix rode Stevens to victory.

Success at the cyclocross world championships, where Stevens riders Niels Albert, Philipp Walsleben, and Hanka Kupfernagel won international acclaim, have added to the brand's mystique. A recent IF Eurobike award for its Ventoux carbon road frame and praise for its light alloy Vuelta frame vindicate Stevens' popularity.

The comfortable, lightweight 7005TB black anodized aluminum Ridge Max Enduro mountain bike frame has 160 mm of spring travel and offers the comfort of a touring Enduro combined with the weight of an all-mountain bike. It has a lowerable Fox Talas RLC fork, X12 through-axle rear section, and post-mount disc brake eyes. It is ideal for uphill biking. A Fox Float RP 23 boost valve, Shimano Deore XT FC-M770-10, QR-20 wheelset with Schwalbe Nobby Nic Evo tires, Oxygen Scorpo-Ridge alloy handlebars, an Oxygen Spark saddle, a Scorpo-Ridge zero offset seatpost, and a Formula The One disc brakeset are other features.

Stevens
Ridge Max

Specialized
S-Works Roubaix SL3 Compact

15 lb (6.8 kg)
$$$
specialized.com

California is the undisputed home of the mountain bike and innovative sports two-wheelers. Mike Sinyard founded Specialized Bicycle Components there in 1974, when, inspired by fine Italian components, he first began to produce his own tires, then a road bike, and then the first production mountain bike, called the Stumpjumper. He went on to introduce Epic, the first carbon-fiber production mountain bike, in 1989. Now Merida Bikes of Taiwan has a stake in the company.

One of the company's more recent models is the fast, smooth S-Works Roubaix SL3, which has a light and stiff Fact 10r carbon frame with a tapered head tube, Fact carbon monocoque fork, vibration-damping Zertz elastomer inserts, and full internal cable routing. The frame won the Paris–Roubaix race with Dura-Ace components, Specialized SL Fact carbon cranks, and DT Tricon tubeless wheels. A light DT Tricon tubeless-ready alloy wheelset allows for lower tire pressure for a better ride. Removable carbon spider and ceramic bearings, plus legendary Shimano Dura-Ace 10-speed shifters add to the bike's performance. S-Works SL ergonomic carbon handlebars are also lightweight. The BG Toupe Plus Expert racing saddle has extra padding for longer rides, plus hollow titanium rails. A Fact carbon Pave seatpost uses a Zertz insert to minimize road vibrations.

Koga
Spyker

28 lb (12.7 kg)
$$$$$
koga.com

Koga, founded in 1974 as Koga-Miyata, is a Dutch manufacturer of high-end race, touring, and trekking bikes that are designed and tested by Koga, and hand-assembled in the Netherlands. The bikes meet stringent performance standards, but, above all, many are simply beautiful. Koga Aeroblade, a 2006 sold-out limited-edition bike for Spyker cars, emulated the high-tech features, wheels, and silver and orange colors of Spyker's endurance racecar, the Aeroblade. This model presaged the new thirst for bikes that echo car brands. Meant for the crew of the former Dutch Spyker factory racing team, the silver and orange bike was produced in a numbered edition of 50. Its features included a titanium frame, an aluminum front fork, wheelset

and mudguards in an aluminum and fiber-glass-coated carbon composite, orange Hulshof luxury leather handlebar grips and saddle, and a special 14-speed Rohloff hub gear transmission. Aeroblade-style wheels, pedals, and leather colors were optional.

Koga
TeeTee Track 2012

10–15 lb (4.5–6.8 kg)
$$$$$
koga.com

Dutch company Koga developed a Kimera Track frameset for Olympic and World Champion sprints by the Netherlands national teams. Koga used a special carbon handlebar stem and seatpost set by Shimano, and gathered input on carbon-fiber structure and geometry from spacecraft engineers and research groups such as TNO in the Netherlands. That know-how helped the Dutch team to win gold at the 2008 Olympics in Beijing and spawned future designs, including this extreme aerodynamic Koga TeeTee Track frameset, developed with sister company Lapierre for the 2012 Dutch team at the Olympics in London. Like an earlier black and blue TeeTee road bike, this version weathered wind-tunnel tests with its fully integrated stem, integrated carbon seatpost with air ducts, streamlined tubing and front fork, and Shimano Di2 system. The high-modulus carbon-fiber frame is extremely light despite the extra-reinforced press-fit bottom bracket. Orange accents the TeeTee Track instead of blue, but the same graphics emphasize speed.

Koga
TeeTee Track 2012

Vanilla
Track Bike

20 lb (9.07 kg)
$$$–$$$$
vanillabicycles.com

Portland, Oregon, is a center for handmade bikes of exceptional quality, and bike craftsman Sacha White may have something to do with that. Since 1999, his Vanilla Bicycles workshop, peopled by fabricators, painters, and other craftspeople, meticulously produces about 50 custom bikes each year that even racing legends like Lance Armstrong vie for. White is the principal designer and frame-builder in the small team. He interviews clients personally, asks them to pedal a trial bike, and plots custom specs on his computer to suit their physique and style. His work, recently featured in a group show at the Museum of Arts and Design in New York, displays refinements such as hand-carved Henry James lugs bonded with silver. Columbus,

Dedacciai, and True Temper strong, lightweight tubular steel frames for Vanilla's touring, city, and track bikes are all bespoke with elements of road bikes, commuter bikes, and off-road bikes melded with retro features and unusual paint colors. Vanilla track frames with jewel-like arabesque joints echo the look of old tractors and vintage motorcycles. Components can include Campagnolo gearsets and Continental tires.

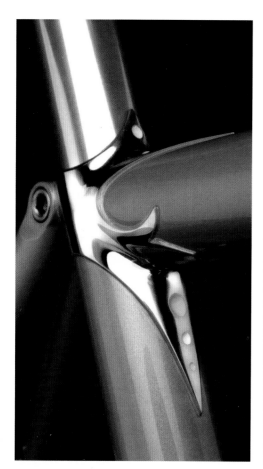

Vanilla
Track Bike

Fuji
Track Ltd 1.0

18 lb (8.16 kg)
$$
fujibike.com

Fuji, named after the famous volcano, was founded in Japan in 1899. A century later, the company thrives in Pennsylvania as an international brand of racing, sports, and urban bikes. Its portfolio ranges from exclusive carbon-frame road bikes such as the pricey Altamira 1.0, as well as affordable beauties such as this specialty Track Ltd 1.0. This bike features a custom-butted oversized 6000 series aluminum-alloy frame with an aerodynamically sculpted down tube, head tube, and seat mast integrated in the main frame, Fuji components, and a standard threaded bottom bracket. The front fork is a carbon FC-770 Fuji straight-blade version with a 11/8-in alloy steerer. Available in many sizes, the stiff yet responsive Track is painted blue and white. The rear triangle

has butted aluminum seatstays, a shaped chainstay, and a replaceable stainless-steel dropout. The Oval W-530T alloy clincher wheelset has Vittoria Zaffiro Pro Slick and Kevlar Bead-Folding tires and flip-flop 700c hubs; silver spokes flank the valve holes. A Tektro forged alloy rear brake, Fuji CGC handlebars and stem, white Fuji Custom Eva tape grips, Fuji PGC clamp for the integrated seatpost, and an Oval SR-700 Sweep saddle with titanium rails add to the ensemble.

Fuji
Track Ltd 1.0

Stevens
Volt Custom Bike

16 lb (7.25 kg)
$$$$
stevensbikes.de

Few companies win accolades as often as Stevens, based in Hamburg, Germany. A wholesaler of premium bike components, Stevens began to produce carbon-and-steel mountain, trekking, and race frames during the 1990s. Police in Hamburg and Canada chose Stevens bikes for their fine suspension; and pro-riders Andreas Kappes and Sascha Henrix, cyclocross world champions Niels Albert, Philipp Walsleben, and Hanka Kupfernagel have all ridden Stevens to victory. A recent IF award for Stevens' Ventoux carbon road frame and praise for its light Vuelta alloy frame vindicate the brand's popularity.

In 2009, Stevens' high-modulus carbon-fiber time-trial Volt custom bike, with its tunnel-tested aerodynamic monocoque design, won accolades at Eurobike. The bike is engineered for speed and has a full carbon F-bend 11 fork, FSA integrated 44 headset, an encased braking system, and integrated seatpost to reduce drag. The sitting angle can be adjusted from 74 to 78 degrees. This triathlon bike is relatively affordable and can be customized with Shimano Dura-Ace D12 or SRAM Red groupsets, a Scorpo carbon T85 wheelset and Continental Competition tires, an Easton Attack TT carbon handlebar and Scorpo stem, a Fi'zi:k Antares carbon saddle, and a Volt carbon seatpost.

Stevens
Volt Custom Bike

Cinelli
XCR Rapha Frame/ Cristal Mirror

8–10 lb (3.62–4.5 kg)
$$$$
cinelli.it

Cinelli, the influential company of 1943 Italian bicycling champion Cino Cinelli, is synonymous with racing. Its aluminum handlebars are the choice of champions. Among its landmark innovations, Cinelli's 1962 Unicantor, the first ever plastic saddle, is still popular. The A. L. Colombo steel tube company acquired Cinelli in 1978 and, now under Gruppo S.R.L., Cinelli continues to make many unique parts. Its XCR frames are made of premium Columbus XCR chromium and molybdenum, and the nickel alloy stainless-steel seamless tubes are triple-butted and welded. The biphasic steel alloy 0.4 mm-thick tube wall is as indestructible as steel, but is lighter and more elastic. The tough frame absorbs vibrations, and its elasticity is ideal for high-speed descents. The 3.15-lb (1.42-kg) XCR's stiffness to weight ratio – better than that of equally expensive aluminum or titanium alloy frames – is news, but its traditional steerer tube and BSA threaded shell makes it a classic-style bike fitted with Columbus carbon monocoque forks and Campagnolo or Shimano components. Handmade in Italy, the limited-edition XCR was made in collaboration with racewear manufacturer Rapha; it features a Cristal Mirror finish and can be customized.

Cinelli
XCR Rapha Frame/
Cristal Mirror

BMX /Mountain

Haro
500-2 freestyle bike

27 lb (12.24 kg)
⚐
harobikes.com

In 1976, Bob Haro, a teenager in Southern California, customized numberplates for top BMX sports racers to fund his own passion for bikes, and soon began to produce his popular plates commercially. Haro, an avid freestyle biker before the sport even had a name, inadvertently founded the genre as he perfected his acrobatic daredevil bike tricks on the road. By the 1980s, catering to the demands of BMX freestylers zipping about from flatland and ramps like he did, Haro launched his Original Haro Freestyler; this remains his namesake company's mainstay in California now that the sport he founded has gone mainstream. Haro bike riders have even won X Games medals. Three decades after its inception, Haro continues to produce tough, affordable bikes, such as the 500 series that champions Ryan Nyquist, Dennis Enarson, or Colin Mackay might ride.

Padded pivotal seats and forged posts, tapered fork legs, CNC-machined stems, a built-in seat clamp, and removable brake and cable mounts go onto a signature chromoly frame with an internal head tube, chromoly forks, handlebars, and cranks, with Haro recycled plastic pedals and Odyssey Aitken tires.

Haro
500-2 freestyle bike

Mercedes-Benz
All-Mountain Mountain Bike

28.2 lb (12.8 kg)
¢¢¢
mercedes-benz-accessories.com

Mercedes-Benz, now under the Daimler AG banner, emerged in 1886 when Karl Benz patented the first petrol-powered car. 125 years later, with a growing interest in healthier, greener complements to cars, Mercedes-Benz is also touting sports and urban bikes, including this full-suspension mountain bike developed with bike manufacturer Rotwild. Its unique conified aluminum alloy 7005 frame has time-tested components such as a Fox Racing F32 RL suspension fork and a DT Swiss suspension strut, each with a spring travel of 4¾ in (120 mm), a 30-speed SRAM X.9 system gear shifter, Shimano HG 74 chain, SRAM crankset, and Wellgo SPD-compatible pedals, hydraulic Avid Elixir 5 disc brakes with a disc diameter of

185 mm, and 26-in DT Swiss X1900 wheels with wide 2.25-in Schwalbe Nobby Continental Attack tires. Like the frame, the saddle post, handlebars, and stem are also by Rotwild. The innovative Fi'zi:k Gobi XM saddle includes ergonomic adjustable features. Lights and mudguards are optional.

Mercedes-Benz
All-Mountain Mountain Bike

Cube
AMS WLS Pro

27 lb (12.24 kg)
$$$
cube.eu

Germany's Cube makes mountain, road, and city bikes, many for women. The strong yet lightweight aluminum AMS WLS Pro full-suspension women's bike has a hydroformed frame with a shorter top tube and a longer steering tube for upright sitting and better pelvic balance. The top bar is lowered for easier mounting. A Fi'zi:k Vesta ergonomic saddle, slimmer handlebars, Ergon GPS-1 non-slip rubber grips, and an RFR Prolight Setback seatpost for a dynamic seating position are among the special components of this size-tuned bike with a four-pivot construction. One pivot located between the dropout and the chainstay ensures that braking or pedaling never impact the rear triangle. More pivots add flexibility for uphill or downhill biking. Other standard components include a Rock Shox Reba RLT U-turn 3½–4¾-in (90–120-mm) motion control with PopLoc fork, a Fox Float RP23 BV 6½ in (165-mm)-length rear shock, a Shimano Deore XT FC-M770-10 Hollowtech press-fit BB 10-speed chainset, Shimano hubs, derailleurs, Formula RX front and rear hydraulic disc brakes, Syntace stem and handlebars, Ergon GPI-S grips, a Fi'zi:k Vesta saddle, an RFR Prolight 1¼-in (31.6-mm) setback seatpost, Schwalbe rims, and Schwalbe Rocket Ron Kevlar Triple Compound 2.25 and Schwalbe Racing Ralph Performance 2.25 tires.

Cube
AMS WLS Pro

Slingshot
BA Blue

22 lb (9.97 kg)
$$-$$$
slingshotbikes.com

Designer Mark Groendal created his "slingshot" suspension system for BMX and mountain bikes in 1980, after he noticed that the fractured down tube on his mini motorbike resulted in smoother rides on rough terrain. He substituted the conventional rigid down tube with a stainless-steel tension cable like those used for sailboats. A hinged joint at the intersection of the top tube and seat tube and compression springs also contributed to shock-damping without affecting speed.

Groendal began producing chromoly steel Slingshots with his brother Joel at their Greendale Bicycle Co. in Wyoming, Michigan. Steel, carbon-fiber, and titanium BMX and mountain racing bikes cemented the brand's reputation, and innovative versions of the bike, including a folding frame, were developed until the company foundered financially. When Aaron Joppe and P.J. McDonald purchased the ailing business from interim owners in 2007, the spring and cable system still prevailed. Typical full hybrid Slingshot bikes, such as BA Blue, have components like Fi'zi:k Aliante road saddles, Velocity wheels, Kenda mountain bike tires, SRAM X-9 derailleurs, Truvativ Stylo cranks, SL-K mountain handlebars and carbon seatposts, and White Brothers Intelligent Magnetic Valve damping forks. John Muenzenmeyer, a former Slingshot TIG welder, joined the new Slingshot team in Grand Rapids, Michigan, where custom bikes ordered online are made.

Slingshot
BA Blue

Breezer
Cloud 9 Pro

27 lbs (12.24 kg)
$$$
breezerbikes.com

Since 1977 mountain bike legend Joe Breeze has been building modern mountain bikes in the Marin Headlands, California. He has led the way with many innovations on his handmade steel frames: uni-crown forks, Breeze-In dropouts, Breezer D'fusion tubing and integrated headsets on his namesake brand of Breezer bikes.

Cloud 9 Pro, his graphite, orange, and white carbon fiber 29-inch wheel hardtail mountain bike, is not the first of its kind, but the detail in its design is extraordinary. Such customized performance bikes, like steeds, have to suit the rider. Yet the curved lines and wider shell design allows anyone to pedal stronger with enough clearance from the tire and chainring. Agility, good climbing, and daredevil thrills on a 29er can only be dampened only by the limits of a rider's skill. Shimano SLX hubs with Centerlock Rotors, Shimano BL-M575 hydraulic disc brakes, a Rock Shox Recon TK Silver fork with a tapered steerer provides some suspension and WTB Laser Disc 29 Trail rims and SLX hubs are other features. Stems, handlebars, and seatpost are all Oval. Although heavier than the Ltd version, this bike is more affordable.

Breezer
Cloud 9 Pro

BMW
Enduro Mountain Bike

32 lb (14.51 kg)
$$$
shop.bmwgroup.com

BMW motorcycles were among the first car companies to add a lightweight suspension fork, first to their motorbike design during the 1990s, and eventually to a mountain bike. The 2011 BMW Cross Country bike and the Enduro Mountain Bike each sport full suspension. The Enduro has four-bar suspension with a Fox Talas 32 RL air-spring fork with as much as 5½ in (140 mm) of give, and Fox RP2 BV shock absorbers with a 5¾-in (145-mm) range. The lightweight aluminum frame, Shimano Deore XT parts, hydraulic disc brakes, and an innovative adjustable angle stem help riders to sit in an optimum position for powerful riding. The bike is produced in metallic shades of white and green, in medium and large sizes.

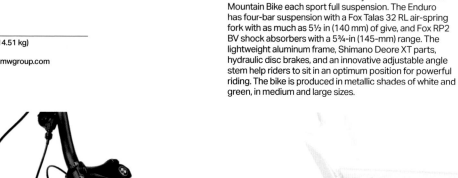

BMW
Enduro Mountain Bike

Lapierre
Froggy 518 Mountain Bike

36 lb (16.32 kg)
$$$$
lapierre-bikes.co.uk

Dijon in France is not just known for producing mustard. It is where Gaston Lapierre started a conventional bike business that, since its inception in 1946, has made the American mountain bike phenomenon of the 1980s its own. Now under its new parent company, Accell Group, Lapierre makes fine freeride and downhill mountain bikes with rear and full suspension systems in collaboration with champions such as Nicolas Vouilloz. The company also sponsors competitive teams, and has become a big presence at Roc d'Azur, the annual international mountain bike mecca.

Lapierre's 2009 Froggy line continues to reign on hard enduro and freeride trails, offering the benefits of OST (Optimized Suspension Technology) suspension that depends on a virtual pivot point and a lighter, rigid hydroformed 7005 aluminum alloy frame with 7 in (180 mm) of rear travel for precise handling and stability on challenging terrain. With OST, the frame adjusts for the rider's weight, and pedaling becomes easier. Quality components for the Froggy 518 include Fox DHX RC4 rear shock, a tapered Fox 36 VAN RC2 fork, Shimano BB with external bearings, Shimano Saint cranksets, Funn Rippa stem, Syncros seatpost and saddle, Funn Fatboy handlebars, Formula RX 8-in (203-mm) brakes, Shimano derailleurs and shifters, and 26-in Alex FR32 wheels with Lapierre hubs and thick Continental Rubber Queen tires.

Lapierre
Froggy 518 Mountain Bike

Monty Bicycles
Kamel 231 XXV

22 lb (9.97 kg)
$$$
monty.es

Spanish trial motorcycle champion Pere Pi stripped a regular bike and added wider handlebars and tires so his young son Ot could experience the trial thrill on a bicycle. That became the prototype for Pi's first Montesita trial bike, manufactured by Montesa Motorcycles in 1981. The new sport of Bike Trial took hold, and Monty Bicycles was born in 1983. Using Monty bikes, Ot Pi and other champions, such as Cesar Cañas and Kazuki Terai, have made BikeTrial an international phenomenon.

Monty's 25th anniversary limited-edition gold and black Kamel 231 XXV with titanium bolts is sharp. Its Monty 7005-T6 aluminum TIG-welded frame with triple-butted tubing, a shock-absorbing humped top tube for stiffness, Monty

6061-T6 fork, 7075 aluminum steerer, FSA Orbit Z internal headset, Monty 6061-T6 welded stem, and Monty 7075-T6 triple-butted riser handlebar with a black and gold anodized finish are among the bike's highlights. For daredevils, welcome upgrades include custom Hope hydraulic disc brakes, FSA ISIS bottom bracket with oversize chromoly spindle and aluminum cups, Monty 7075-T6 ISIS-forged and CNC-machined cranks, and Monty 6061-T5 26-in rims with Monty Maxxis Mobster and Minion tires.

Monty Bicycles
Kamel 231 XXV

Ibis
Mojo HD (Heavy Duty)

25–28 lb (11.3–12.7 kg)
$$$$
ibiscycles.com

Scot Nicol, a pioneering mountain biker, founded Ibis in Mendocino, California, in 1981 when a friend asked him to build a frame. The company has become famous for its carbon-fiber mountain bikes, although it also produces relatively affordable multipurpose bikes, such as the noted Hakkalugi line. An obsession with ever-stronger and ever-lighter bikes has produced the Mojo SL-R. However, an earlier iteration of a similar frame, the Mojo HD, which took Ibis' resident champion Brian Lopes to recent victory, is shown here for its versatility as a hardtail cross-country bike with the added comfort of dw-link suspension for difficult off-road trails.

The bike's sinewy shape and exposed carbon weave along the top tube are beautiful details (produced in China), but its stiffness, light weight, and ability to absorb hard pedaling uphill, rocks, roots, and drops downhill, and the Mojo HD's adjustable seatpost, short wheelbase, and 67-degree head angle result in a bike with dual qualities fit for trail and mountain. 26-in wheels, 12 x 5½-in (142-mm) Maxle rear axle, Fox RP23 shocks, post-mount forged magnesium left dropout, direct-mount front derailleur, and other optional features mean the bike can add up to about 25 lb (11.3 kg) along with the 6.3-pound (2.85-kg) frame.

Ibis
Mojo HD (Heavy Duty)

Ibis
Mojo HD (Heavy Duty)

Specialized
P.2

20 lb (9.07 kg)
$ $
specialized.com

Mike Sinyard, who founded Specialized in 1974, was a globe-trotting cycling enthusiast. He brought back Italian handlebars and stems as souvenirs from his travels, and began to produce fine bike parts including tires, a road bike, and the first production mountain bike, called the Stumpjumper. He introduced Epic, the first carbon-fiber production mountain bike in 1989. Now Merida Bikes of Taiwan – a huge company nearly as large as Giant Bicycles and Trek Bicycle Corporation, holds a big stake in his California-based company.

BMX freestyle bike aficionados lean to Specialized's single-speed P2, with its Reynolds 520 chromoly butted tubing and integrated head tube, for its durability.

The tough chromoly frames ward off fatigue and abrasion on dirt jumps. Cranks are located at the mid-bottom bar, and 3D-forged horizontal dropouts with a chain tensioner are ideal for dirt, park, or street. An X Fusion Enix R fork has hydraulic damping with 3⅛ in (80 mm) of compression. Low-flange, 36-spoke double-wall 26-in alloy wheels with sealed cartridge bearings complement Specialized tires. Smaller wheels can be fitted. A BMX-style three-piece tubular chromoly crankset, single-speed 25-tooth chainring, Avid Elixir 1 hydraulic disc brakes, riser handlebars, and a molded P. Combo saddle and alloy seatpost complete the lightweight bike.

SE
PK Ripper

25 lb (11.3 kg)
⚡
sebikes.com

Scot Breithaupt, a 1970s BMX pioneer, started racing at age 14. He went on to launch a BMX PR firm called Scot Enterprises, and eventually set up a bike company with the shortened moniker of SE Racing. He experimented with flat/oval aluminum alloy tubular framing that he dubbed "Floval." These thicker, flattened down tubes and top tubes are now characteristic of modern BMX bicycles. Aluminum is a difficult metal to shape into bicycle frames because, if handled incorrectly during production, it can become fragile. Breithaupt's PK Ripper was the first mass-produced aluminum BMX bicycle that could be relied on for racing and was affordable; it became the BMX to have because of its strength and lightness. The modern iteration of the PK Ripper is still manufactured by SE (now called Sports Engineering) Racing and distributed by Advanced Sports, Inc.

SE
Quadangle Looptail

27 lb (12.24 kg)
$
sebikes.com

Scot Breithaupt's Scot Enterprises (SE) recently revived one of its 1980s BMX classics, the 24-in Quadangle Looptail in a black, individually numbered version. It has chromoly tubing, a classic double down tube, looptail rear, and retro dropouts. Other features include chromoly Landing Gear forks and SE 3PCE chromoly steel cranks, a sealed US bottom bar and Splined axle, a 39T alloy chainring/17T freewheel, and 36H alloy sealed hubs. The bike also comes equipped with Alex DM24 double-wall rims, alloy V-brake, alloy fluted seatpost, and chromoly handlebars with S-1E retro grips and retro pads.

Specialized
S-Works Epic Carbon 29 SRAM

22 lb (9.97 kg)
$¢$
specialized.com

Mike Sinyard's Specialized produces this full-suspension, super-light carbon-fiber S-Works Epic, the first 29er to win a World Cup event. With SRAM's XX component group, sealed cartridge-bearing pivots, 142-mm dropouts and 100-mm travel suspension, this is a solid competitive XC bike. It has a Specialized/Fox remote Mini-Brain inertia-valve shock absorber with Kashima coating that allows seamless transitions from soft pedaling on smooth terrain to fast action on rougher ground. It has a carbon/crown steerer tube, Roval Control SL 29 wheelset with carbon rims, and DT Swiss spokes for a stiff, durable, light, and fast bike. Its custom Avid XX World Cup R magnesium brakes are light for powerful cross-country rides with two-piece rotors,

alloy-backed semi-metallic pads, carbon levers, and titanium hardware. S-Works XC carbon flat handlebars, Specialized grips, and carbon cranksets are other features.

Van Nicholas
Zion Rohloff

22 lb (9.97 kg)
$$$
vannicholas.com

Until carbon fiber appeared on the scene, titanium was the material of choice for performance bikes. At Van Nicholas, the Dutch bike frame-building firm that has offered complete custom-built bikes online since 1999, they have bucked the trend and still favor titanium's intrinsic beauty, strength, light weight, non-corrosive, and easy-to-repair qualities. The company uses titanium exclusively for every hand-polished frame that it builds and guarantees for life.

Van Nicholas has produced the relatively affordable Zion Rohloff, a hardtail bike with front suspension meant for XC marathons and racing, but adaptable for all-mountain and off-road freestyle riding.

Zion's geometry for slightly upright riding is designed for a variety of road conditions and for optimum comfort. The frame is optimized for a shorter 4-in (100-mm) travel fork for regular uphill or downhill trail and single-track riding while a suite of braze-ons allows for any kind of braking system you prefer, including disc brakes. Zion is also meant for touring, and its smooth, ultra-slick enclosed 14-gear Rohloff option keeps the dirt out.

City
/Utility

Frost Produkt
Alta

25–27 lb (11.3–12.24 kg)
$$$
altabikes.no

Alta is a simply beautiful bike realized by a team of industrial, furniture, and graphic designers. Oslo-based furniture designers Norway Says and graphic designers Bleed collaborated with design consultancy Frost Produkt on this 20-lb (9.07-kg) limited-edition, single-speed urban bike. It became so popular that it went into serial production almost immediately after it appeared in 2006. Light, timeless, fast, durable bikes for city use – hybrids between classic couriers and mountain bikes intended to jump curbs and potholes alike – have, after Alta, become the new vogue. Alta's aluminum frame and signature handlebars promote a leaning posture for a rocking motion while climbing in San Francisco or riding out urban pitfalls in New York. Now in the permanent collection of the Norwegian National Museum, this bike has spawned cousins in Australia, the United States, and Japan.

Van Nicholas
Amazon Rohloff

26 lb (11.79 kg)
$$$$
vannicholas.com

Van Nicholas, the Dutch bike frame-building firm, has always favored titanium as the ideal material and it is now more affordable than ever. Van Nicholas founder Jan-Willem Sintnicolaas guarantees all his hand-polished titanium frames for life. Delivery is within a couple of weeks.

The Amazon Rohloff, a practical street commuter bike with a plain-gauge titanium tubular frame, features an enclosed 14-gear Rohloff hub for smooth, almost unnoticeable shifting and much lower maintenance on an already maintenance-free diamond frame that comes in various customizable sizes.

The CNC-sculpted dropouts are attractive. A Bushnell bottom bracket, instead of slotted dropouts, helps to make the chain taut, and although there are no disc brake mounts, the Amazon has a rear rack and mudguard braze-ons, cable stops, and guides for the Rohloff hub. A Brooks B17 Normal leather saddle, Van Nicholas Ti setback seatpost, DRC wide 700c 32/32 three-cross butted wheels with stainless-steel spokes, high-density Schwalbe Marathon Supreme tires, Truvativ Stylo GXP 7-in (175-mm) 42-tooth chainset, Shimano cantilever brakesets, a carbon belt drive, or KMC 3/32 chain and VNT carbon alloy forks, are all options.

Velorbis
Arrow Gent's Bike

27 lb (12.2 kg)
$$$$$
velorbis.com

Velorbis, a brand of classic European-style sit-up bikes founded in 2006 by two Scandinavian entrepreneurs in Copenhagen, sources fine European components and manufactures frames in Germany. The brand's signature head badge of a chromed aluminum crowned-rampant lion head alludes to a regal European past and old-world quality. However, among the latest designs is a sporty urban single-speed city bike called Arrow. The classic lines of its black powder-coated and rust-protected lugged chromoly steel frame have a contemporary pared-down sensibility. The weather-resistant zinc-plated fenders are slender, and the bike's standard features include a sturdy brown leather sports saddle and Brooks English leather handle grips, stainless-steel rims, SRAM or Shimano Nexus coaster brakes, a Sturmey-Archer crankset and slim 1¼-in (27-mm) black Schwalbe tires. It has no rear carrier, but a special brown leather messenger bag is designed for storage space.

Velorbis
Arrow Gent's Bike

Joey Ruiter
Big City Cruiser

30–32 lb (13.6–14.51 kg)
$$
jruiter.com

Award-winning industrial designer Joey Ruiter, from Michigan, hoped to win $250,000 with his bicycle design when it was entered in an international competition called Art Prize. As spare as a minimalist painting or a hobby horse, because it is intended for narrow spaces in inner cities, the chainless Big City Cruiser looks incomplete. It is pared down to an essential frame, a rear wheel with pedals, and a front wheel with a disc brake. It is not fast, and it is tiring to ride over long distances, but it handles well, is good for café hopping, and with rear wheel power it can whip over curbs easily. It starts, stops, and sits well on its 29-in rims with thick tires. Ruiter describes his rear hub details with haiku clarity: "Planetary internal freewheeling, unicycle through axle."

Joey Ruiter
Big City Cruiser

Public
C7 City Bike

25 lb (11.3 kg)
$
publicbikes.com

San Francisco's vertiginous hills inspired Rob Forbes, the founder of furniture company Design Within Reach, to launch Public, a company that brings lightweight bicycles to practical commuters. Public's chromoly steel frames are sturdier than aluminum frames, yet lighter than most of the 45-lb (20.41-kg) vintage Dutch and French frames they resemble. Five frame types in bright orange, black, and a few other colors with signature stripes include the C7, an affordable orange or cream 7-speed step-through version with handlebars designed for upright cycling and better visibility. Sleek steel mud fenders, aluminum chainguards, a simplified Revo Twist gear shifter and one-size-fits-all reinforced resin pedals make Public's C7 bicycle ideal for urban riders. The bike's 1½-in (35-mm) tires on lightweight alloy rims can take on hills, curbs, and potholes without sacrificing speed, while optional rear racks or front baskets make them great workhorses too. An internal hub and low-profile gears instead of standard Shimano derailleurs are available upgrades.

Public
C7 City Bike

Velorbis
Churchill Balloon and Victoria Classic

36 lb (16.32 kg)
\$\$
velorbis.com; mydutchbike.com

Classic designs, such as England's Tony Pashley bikes and Dutch Grandpa bikes, are making a comeback; makers of the finest of the "new classics" include Copenhagen-based Velorbis. According to Velorbis (Bicycle Rotation) founding partner Ken Bødiker, the Danish company, set up in 2006, was a response to London's subway bombings in 2007, which temporarily left Londoners without public transportation. Based on European diamond-frame upright bikes with high handlebars, Velorbis bikes are handmade in Germany and harken back to pre-war years. The Churchill Balloon for men and the step-through Victoria Classic for women each have black powder-coated rust-protected lugged chromoly steel frames. Standard features include weather-resistant chainguards, slender zinc-plated fenders, polished stainless-steel handlebars, brown English leather Brooks saddles, leather handle grips and mud flaps, stainless-steel rims, polished chrome bells, front Sturmey-Archer dynamo hub and drum brake or SRAM T3 coaster brakes, Sturmey-Archer 5-speed rear hub and drum brake or Shimano Nexus 7-speed hubs, dynamo-driven Busch & Müller lights, Van Schothorst and BOMI components, Schwalbe Fat Frank balloon tires for Churchill and Delta Cruiser tires with reflector sides for Victoria, a practical rear carrier, Basta locks, enclosed hub driven lights, and a kickstand.

Velorbis
Churchill Balloon and
Victoria Classic

Velorbis
Churchill Balloon and
Victoria Classic

Giant Bicycles
CitySpeed

35 lb (15.87 kg)
\$\$
michael-young.com; giant-bicycles.com

Giant, the behemoth Taiwanese bike manufacturer, produces predictable albeit well-engineered bikes that are designed for mass-consumption. This makes CitySpeed noteworthy; the fashionable 8-speed urban bike, designed by British industrial designer Michael Young for Giant, handily won Eurobike's Gold Award in 2008.

Young and his design team created a sleek yet classic diamond frame of ALUXX hydroformed aluminum tubing that incorporates subtle enhancements, including LED headlights, a battery, and a clock with timer and stopwatch functions housed in a cavity within the aluminum mountain bike-type flat handlebar, a battery-operated rear light that can be attached beneath the saddle, or on an optional

rear rack. For easier long-distance pedaling, Young slightly canted the anti-slip pedals outward; the powder-coated city bike (now only available in white and with several component substitutions) looks sporty. Young opted for straight advanced-grade composite with alloy steerer forks. The latest CitySpeed CS versions (unlike the award-winner shown here) have a Giant Sport Road saddle, internal Shimano Alfine 8-speed hub gears, Giant Root Hydraulic disc brakes, an FSA 306 44T crankset, and Giant CR70 DW aluminum wheels with stainless-steel spokes and Kenda Kwick Roller tires.

Giant Bicycles
CitySpeed

Elian Cycles
Commuter

28 lb (12.7 kg)
$$$-$$$$$
eliancycles.com

In Utrecht, the Netherlands town where De Stijl architect Gerrit Rietveld's historic Schröder House is noted for its pared-down beauty, bike mechanic Elian Jamal Veltman makes equally understated classics in collaboration with moonlighting web designer Wilco Drost. Hand-built Elian cycles have simple, strong, yet flexible fillet-brazed chromoly steel frames with matching seat stems. These single-speed commuter bikes have elegant, triple-triangle frames created by incorporating the seatstays – a technique first seen on GT bikes – to add strength as well as visual interest. The sporty lines of the frame and its parts have the visceral appeal of a track bike. However, with quality Campagnolo cranks and chainring, Sugino crankset, Sturmey-Archer

hubs, KMC chain, Duomatic gears with a 2-speed hub with coaster brake, and Panaracer tires, this is not just any track bike. Mounts provided for front and rear brakes and other additional touches make each bike customizable.

Elian Cycles
Commuter

Vanilla
Commuter Bike

28 lb (12.7 kg)
$$$-$$$$$
vanillabicycles.com

In Portland, Oregon, former messenger Sacha White has a reputation for exacting, artful bike craftsmanship. Since 1999, his Vanilla Bicycles workshop, peopled by fabricators, painters, and other craftspeople, meticulously produces about 50 custom bikes each year. White is the principal designer and frame-builder in the small team. His work, recently featured in a group show at the Museum of Arts and Design in New York, displays refinements such as hand-carved Henry James lugs bonded with silver. Columbus, Dedacciai, and True Temper strong, lightweight tubular steel frames for Vanilla touring, city, and track bikes are all bespoke with elements of road bikes, commuter bikes, and off-road bikes with retro features and unusual paint colors.

Dependable Vanilla commuter bikes integrate fenders, lights, and racks with as much care as is lavished on track frames. An English Brooks leather saddle, Hutchinson Top Speed tires, a double kickstand, a fixed rear carrier rack, and polished alloy handlebars are all options.

Vanilla
Commuter Bike

Puch
Crunch 1899 7s

35 lb (15.87 kg)
⚡
puch-fietsen.nl

In 1899, in Graz, Austria, Johann Puch founded a tiny namesake bike company that grew to include motorbikes. The company was conscripted to make arms during World Wars I and II, but reverted to bike manufacturing in more settled times. During the 1970s, Puch produced some of the first BMX bikes in Europe and even sponsored BMX racers in the United States. A subsidiary of Cycleurope since 1997, Puch now produces millions of city bikes, including this elegant throwback, the Puch Crunch 1899 7s transport cruiser bike. The oversized 3-speed black aluminum bike with Hi-Ten forks is equipped with a black aluminum front carrier, Shimano Nexus and Coaster brakes, 26-in wheels with black rims and white Spectra Special tires, VP558 pedals, an adjustable aluminum stem topped by a brown Spectra Beach Cruiser Royal saddle, Retro BL 112 and Spectra saddle LED lights, an AXA solid lock, and plastic cruiser mudguards.

Audi
Duo City

25–32 lb (11.3–14.51 kg)
$$$$
audi-collection.com/Cycling

Carmakers have dabbled with bike design on and off, but never as seriously as now. Audi went further by teaming up with Portland, Oregon's Renovo Hardwood Bicycles to produce Duo, the first all-hardwood hollow monocoque frame for sport, road, and urban riders. The frames parts are computer-cut, heat-epoxy-bonded and hand-finished. The wood, a sustainable choice, is tested for reliability and guaranteed. The light- or dark-colored wood frames are artfully crafted, but also built to perform well. Wood absorbs shocks and vibration better than metals and carbon fiber, according to Renovo's Ken Wheeler, a former airplane designer. It is also lighter – one cubic inch of wood is about one-fourth the weight of aluminum – and stiffer.

All Duo bikes feature a Gates center-track belt drive, aluminum and carbon fiber forks and handlebars, disc brakes, and LED lighting. Duo City is the most versatile and affordable of the bikes, with wider tires and a Shimano Nexus 8-speed internal hub gear. It is designed for upright seating, and the 25-lb (11.3-kg) frame can be fitted with fenders, a rack, and dynamo lights, which, of course, will add more weight.

Urban Arrow
Electric Assist Cargo Bike

45 lb (20.41 kg)
$$–$$$
urbanarrow.com

Award-winning designer Wytze van Mansum's design for Urban Arrow, a firm launched by entrepreneurs Gerald van Weel and Jorrit Kreek in Amsterdam, updates the typical Dutch bakfiets or work/transport bike. A low center of gravity makes its sturdy aluminum frame extremely stable. Not yet in full production, it will contain an integrated motor and chain, and a dynamo hub for lights. Designed for families with children that want to have a greener alternative to gas-greedy SUVs, the pedelec uses high-end components and a sturdy, lightweight, recyclable molded foam box as the carriage for little people or up to 375 lb (170 kg) of cargo. Curved tubes around the top of the box protect the edges as well as children's fingers from accidents. It is possible to remove the box to transform the bike front into a flatbed carrier for a lidded box. The bike can also be converted to a trike. Even without a full load, the bike is heavy, and without an electrical boost it would be good only on flat terrain. A powerful German-made electric pedal assist motor boosts the back wheel and in first gear it surges forward silently, ready for any hill. Daum controls on the handlebars monitor the speed. Kids can go in and out of the low carriage without tipping it over, while other handy details, designed by Renske Solkesz, include integrated cup holders, grocery nets, and a rain cover. A fixed bolt saddle post is an anti-theft feature, and wide, puncture-resistant balloon tires tackle city roads easily.

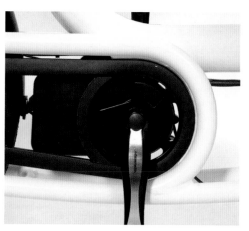

Urban Arrow
Electric Assist Cargo Bike

Urban Arrow
Electric Assist Cargo Bike

Fuji
Feather

22 lb (9.97 kg)
✢
fujibike.com

Bike company Fuji, founded in Japan in 1899, now distributes racing and urban bikes from Pennsylvania, including this very attractive, affordable, fixed-gear Feather inspired by classic 700c track bikes. Its short wheelbase and polished aluminum components highlight a retro red, black, white, or gold-painted Elios 2 custom-butted chromoly steel frame with an outer butted seat tube that can be converted to a single-speed bike with brakes, since it is pre-drilled for cabling and accessories. A custom-triple-butted chromoly steel fork crown is drilled for front brakes if needed, and serviceable Wellgo Road pedals with clips and straps can be upgraded too. The Fuji chromoly axle sealed bearing with track nut hubs, Fuji double-wall, high-profile (pothole-worthy) rims with 36 holes, Kenda 25c tires, Promax brakeset, Fuji 6061 butted road drop handlebars with Fuji keirin grips, and Fuji super-light racing saddle give this all-purpose urban bike its simple, sporty look. A 46-tooth Fuji Track forged alloy chainset supported by a rear 16-tooth sprocket on a sealed alloy track flip-flop hub makes the gear ratio ideal for commuters.

Fuji
Feather

Umberto Dei
Giubileo

30 lb (13.6 kg)
↔
umbertodei.it

Umberto Dei's eponymous company was founded in 1896, and is among Italy's oldest bicycle producers. Of their many city and commuter bike designs, most sport classic details from the 1930s. Umberto Dei's artisans fashion vintage-style bikes by hand, but they are, mechanically speaking, state-of-the-art. The Giubileo's cocoa- or moss-green-colored brazed and lugged steel frame for both sexes has a steel fork with chromed steel Chiavelli cranks, aluminum handlebars, rear carrier, aluminum sports brakes, aluminum alloy wheels with black 26-in Michelin tires, anodized aluminum hubs, stainless-steel fenders, a closed chain case, leather Dei saddle and hand-sewn handgrips, chrome dynamo lights, a ding-dong bell, and a frame-mounted wheel lock.

Umberto Dei
Giubileo

Boardman
Hybrid Pro 10 Urban

20 lb (9.07 kg)
♻♻
boardmanbikes.com

Gold medalist Chris Boardman has been in Great Britain's professional cycling limelight on- and off-stage, at the Olympics, World Championships, and Commonwealth Games, as a television commentator for the BBC and Europort, and at the research and development helm of his eponymous bike company, where he has initiated winning-performance improvements in a wide range of excellent road, mountain, CX, and women's bikes. He hasn't skimped on providing a road and off-road urban hybrid either. The Boardman Hybrid Pro 10 has high-end road race and mountain bike specs: flat handlebars, a triple-butted super-light aluminum alloy welded tube frame with a tapered steerer, and a diamond-to-round top tube for stiffness,

an ultralight carbon fork, SRAM 10-speed Rival gearing, Avid Elixir 5 brakes including a caliper-mounted rear disc brake, an FSA Energy Compact BB30 chainset, and Ritchley Pro Disc wheels. The curved wishbone seatstays offer enhanced comfort. Add mudguards and a rear rack, and the racer becomes an extraordinary commuter.

Biomega
LDN (London)

25–27 lb (11.3–12.24 kg)
$$$
biomega.dk

To Biomega's line of chainless bikes, British industrial designer Ross Lovegrove added another, LDN (London), as a homage to his hometown. Lovegrove, always fascinated by nature and organic shapes, looked at wishbones for inspiration when he designed the frame, although all essential components, including the 26-in wheels, are made of carbon fiber. The laminated monocoque structure is very strong but it is light – about 20 lb (9.07 kg). A slot in the wide down tube (which is also the top bar) helps to make the 8-speed LDN lighter and easier to store on a wall. An innovative shaft drive instead of a chain makes the design all the more minimal.

Sögreni
Louisiana (Sögreni Classic)

30 lb (13.6 kg)
$$-$$$
sogrenibikes.com

In 1980s Copenhagen, a young Søren Sögreni stumbled into bike-making when he could not find a model he liked so decided to make one himself. "I found normal bikes boring," he says. Before long, he was making bikes for friends. He salvaged the best parts from old castaways and designed new ones. "I improved the things that people always said broke first," Sögreni says. "I made the bell on my bikes simple. I made the smallest lamps of aluminum, brass, and copper."

Sögreni has been producing classic bikes with custom details ever since. Wheels, a limited-edition silver alloy bike made for the Georg Jensen silver company in 2008, came with a handcrafted silver bell. Bikes for Bang & Olufsen, for the Swedish company Källemo, and for Conran shops also feature in Sögreni's repertoire.

Louisiana, the Danish museum of modern art, invited Søren Sögreni to design a bicycle for the museum that is now in the museum's collection. Also called the Sögreni Classic, the single-speed Louisiana bike has just the basics without gears or extras. A Brooks saddle, handgrips of Polish leather, low handlebars for wind-resistance, a Sögreni bell, handmade pedals and fenders, a mounted lock, a handy kickstand, optional SRAM gearsets for the single-speed or 3- and 9-gear options, disc brakes, and 28-in wheels add distinction.

Sögreni
Louisiana (Sögreni Classic)

Schindelhauer Bikes
Ludwig XI

25 lb (11.3 kg)
$$$
schindelhauerbikes.com

Some years ago, Jörg Schindelhauer, a German mechanical engineer, teamed up with engineer Manuel Holstein, economist Martin Schellhase, and industrial designer Stephan Zehren to design a sports car. Instead, as if anticipating the surge in urban riding, they formed Schindelhauer Bikes to create hybrids with roots in track, sports, and messenger bikes for comfortable upright riding and speed. They adapted a standard diamond frame by cutting its rear triangle and installing a locking system for a carbon-belt drive that is now patented. This innovation won them a 2010 Red Dot award.

Since then, hundreds of 6061 aluminum-alloy, TIG-welded, triple-butted hand-assembled track, sport,

touring, and mountain bikes have left their factory. The bikes range in price from moderately expensive to very expensive, and have Germanic names such as Lotte, Viktor, Siegfried, and Ludwig.

The distinctive unpainted all-aluminum Ludwig XI touring bike has a silent, greaseless Gates Carbon Drive belt, a leather Brooks saddle, an 11-speed Shimano Alfine hub, Rapidfire shifters, Schindelhauer Ergo antique brown hand pedal leather grips, an integrated Tange Seiki headset, tough Continental City Ride tires with reflex stripes and quick-release catches, Alexrims G6000, a Hollowtech crankset, Tektro-forged aluminum dual-pivot brakes, an integrated Kalloy seatpost, and aluminum forks.

Schindelhauer Bikes
Ludwig XI

Schindelhauer Bikes
Ludwig XI

Trek
Mendota

30 lb (13.6 kg)
$$$
trekbikes.com

Gary Fisher was the San Francisco Bay Area teenager who coined the term "mountain bike" and launched a new sport; he is now realizing an old dream: to get more people out of cars and on to bikes. His Gary Fisher Collection bikes for Trek, the global American brand headquartered in Wisconsin, include honest, sturdy, and inexpensive machines for urban riding. Trek, as ubiquitous in the United States as Batavus bikes are in Holland, began in 1976 about the time Fisher was creating his first mountain bike. His new mat black Mendota bike in the Fast City series for Trek is intended for practical daily commuting, to get around short distances, or for exercise. Its squared tubular aluminum frame has flip-flop dropouts to change gears,

hubs, or brakes easily, and has a lightweight Bontrager Satellite Elite carbon disc fork. Bontrager SSR disc wheels with Race all-weather hard-case tires, a 9-speed Shimano drivetrain, M590 Deore front derailleur, and a M662 SLX in the rear, Shimano M443 Octalink cranks, Wellgo alloy cage pedals with clips and straps, a Bontrager H2 Flex Form saddle, Bontrager seatpost, handlebar, and Satellite Plus ergonomic grips, and a Slimstak sealed headset with Avid BB5 mechanical disc brakes come as standard features.

Koga
Miyata Leontien

44 lb (19.95 kg)
$$
koga.com

Koga's homage to Leontien van Moorsel, one of the most successful Dutch athletes and an Olympic medalist, is a quality city bike called Leontien. It is not remotely a super-lightweight sports bike, but it is built for ease of use by women and for safety.

The Leontien's hand-built triple-hardened and triple-butted TIG-welded 7005 aluminum tube frame includes a top tube combined with a new twin tube and an elevated chainstay. The down tube has an integrated brake and shifter cable. An integrated Tange Seiki ZS-22 headset, built-in attachment point for all accessories, and an unusual chain adjuster adds to the bike's appeal. An Insync Odesa LX front fork, Selle San Marco leather grips, Look In M-flex saddle, Shimano CN NX10 chain, Shimano brakeset and cranks, 28-in Koga rims with Continental tires and tubes, Koga VP191 pedals, a De Woerd chainguard, a hub dynamo, LED headlights and rear lights, mudguards and coatguards, a rear carrier, an AXA Defender ring lock, and a Pletscher kickstand all add reliability and weight. A multifunctional Koga shoulder/bike bag is a smart accessory. Colors include a Dutch orange and pearlized white combination, shown here.

Puma
Mopion

55 lb (24.94 kg)
$$
puma-bikes.com

Copenhagen-based design firms KiBiSi and Biomega have added to Puma's range of bicycles with a fashionable cargo bike for hauling groceries or slightly bigger loads. Smooth steering for deft maneuvering around cities makes the lightweight aluminum Mopion frame practical for commuters as well. The extra-large front carrier complements the well-balanced bike's elongated shape. The handlebar reach is such that riders can lean slightly forward but in a head-up position for navigating easily. Mopion, named after an island in the Atlantic, is awash with ideas from both sides of the pond, borrowing equally from European diamond-frame commuter and urban bike designs and the colorful boldness of American sports bikes.

Bella Ciao
Neorealista and Moscova

25–27 lb (11.3–12.24 kg)
$$–$$$
bellaciao.de

With its roots in classic Italian bicycle design and its Northern Italian handcrafted frames, the German bicycle company Bella Ciao describes its slender powder-coated steel or Columbus Thron tube set and limited-edition all-chrome steel frames as "la poesia della libertia." The "poetry of freedom" that Bella Ciao founder Matthias Maier refers to is best expressed in the simplicity of the Neorealista design, with its polished stainless-steel Gilles Berthoud fenders and single-speed coaster brake configuration. The polished aluminum handlebars are proprietorial, echoing vintage Cinelli. Shimano Nexus 3-speed coaster brakes or Sturmey-Archer Duomatic coaster brakes and a Sturmey-Archer Duomatic 2-speed hub operated by kick shift are

all optional. Assembled in Germany, the Neorealista or the higher-end Neorealista Veloce step-throughs have become the company's mainstay. A very limited-edition version of this bike, the Moscova, celebrates minimalism with its startlingly elegant chrome finish, Brooks leather seats, and weather-resistant Italian leather grips. Lacking a chainguard, the Moscova seems lighter and more ephemeral. Corvo Citta Uomo and Monza are equivalent men's versions.

Bella Ciao
Neorealista and Moscova

Vanmoof
No. 5

31 lb (14.06 kg)
⇕
vanmoof.com

In Holland, where even the royal family rides bikes, the taste for sturdy yet attractive two-wheelers in cities is ever-growing. Vanmoof, an Amsterdam bike brand run by two brothers, Taco and Ties Carlier, offers startlingly fresh, no-frills designs by Sjoerd Smit. Selling stylish, affordable, simple, and durable bikes is the company's aim.

Smit, an industrial designer, adapted the classic triangular Dutch bike frame geometry, and engineered his thick-walled tubular anodized aluminum all-weather Vanmoof frame, meant for daily use, with the latest wireless technology. "We wanted the bike to be easy to use and vandal-proof. All accessories such as fenders and lights could be integrated into the frame," he explains.

In the latest Vanmoof models, solar-powered LED lights and USB ports embedded in the frames can be activated with the swipe of a keycard. Easy to lift, all five models that the company offers are designed for upright riding, and go faster than you might expect. A coaster brake, a hidden steel chain lock by Abus, integrated cabling, a broad handlebar, and a classic Brooks leather seat complement each frame's minimalist look. No. 5, complete with all the latest integrated Vanmoof innovations, is a Red Dot award-winner.

Biomega
NYC (New York City)

25–27 lb (11.3–12.24 kg)
$$
biomega.dk

In keeping with its first distinctive chainless bicycle, CPN (Copenhagen), Danish firm Biomega's NYC bike is a tribute to another biking capital, New York. Designed by KiBiSi – a collaborative industrial design consultancy co-founded by Biomega's Jens Martin Skibsted, architect Bjarke Ingels of BIG architects, and designer Lars Holme Larsen of Kilo Design – NYC has a conventional diamond frame of welded aluminum with a slyly integrated mudguard located on the down tube. Straightforward and low-key, NYC also has a visible, albeit greaseless and silent, carbon-fiber belt drive, Shimano 8-speed hub gears and disc brakes. The bike is fitted with 26-in wheels.

Retrovelo
Otto

35 lb (15.87 kg)
$$$
retrovelo.de; mydutchbike.com

Although Retrovelo (see pages 130 and 213) celebrates traditional silhouettes and craftsmanship, the more modern designs in their repertoire nod to tricked-out messenger bikes and utilitarian city bikes, as well as mountain bikes. Retrovelo adapted their Ponyvelo chassis with a Schlumpf 2-speed bottom bracket gearbox to create the feisty Otto town bike in a single-speed (shown) or double-speed version with an expanded steerer tube for strength and a more solid look for its chromoly steel diamond frame with BMX handlebars. A distinctive triple-plate fork connection is a signature detail for Retrovelo. Vertical dropouts with disc brake mounts are combined with the eccentric bottom bracket to control chain tension, and the Avid BB7 disc brake system is easier to maintain than hydraulic brakes. The 24-in (61-mm) wheelset's gearbox is activated with the click of the heel to shift gears. The bike also comes with a Selle Vintage Rolls saddle.

Retrovelo
Otto

Seven
Parcour S

12 lb (5.44 kg)
$$$$
sevencycles.com

Seven Cycles founder Rob Vandermark and his team have been making custom-butted and straight-gauge seamless titanium bicycle frames, alongside high-modulus carbon-fiber, filament-wound carbon fiber, and steel, road, track, mountain, and tandem bikes in Massachusetts since 1997. A custom titanium stem and mountain bike handlebar, a carbon-fiber road fork, as well as aluminum handlebars, stems, and seatposts made on site distinguish Seven bikes, which can be ordered off the shelf or customized. Options such as cable routing, water-bottle mounts, paint color, and decal color at no additional charge make the offerings unique. Seven selects the right tube diameter and wall thickness to suit a rider's weight, age, and riding terrain, and builds every frame to order. Reaming, chasing, machining, welding, finishing, and painting are done under one roof. All this explains why Seven bikes are not cheap; even the Seven Parcour S, a beautiful fixed-gear commuter bike with Integrity straight-gauge titanium framing and handlebars, carbon fork, fenders, track dropouts, and special sandblasted decals, comes with a hefty price tag. It won't rust, even if you leave it outside all year long. A Brooks leather saddle, Mavic 26-in or 29-in wheels, Michelin tires, and SRAM Omnium cranks are other options.

Retrovelo
Paula

35 lb (15.87 kg)
$$
retrovelo.de; mydutchbike.com

At Retrovelo in Germany, Frank Patitz and Matthias Mehlert emphasize a link to traditional silhouettes and handmade craft. Paula, an old-fashioned Dutch-style step-through with a lugged chromoly steel frame, is designed for upright city cycling. It is updated with Shimano 7- or 8-speed internal gear hubs, a Shimano brakeset, a hub generator for Busch & Müller Lumotec retro chromed headlights and an LED-seculite tail light, a Brooks leather saddle B67s/B68s, ESGE center stand, stainless-steel fenders, optional rear rack, and hand-built wheelsets. These features are complemented with custom Fat Frank balloon tires made by Schwalbe for Paula (and Paul, the male equivalent) bikes to sail over road bumps, curbs, and streetcar rails.

Puma
Pico

27 lb (12.24 kg)
$
puma-bikes.com

A European Consumer Choice winner, the Pico bike from German sports shoe brand Puma is one of several designs made in collaboration with design firms Biomega and KiBiSi, both of which are based in Copenhagen, Denmark. The Pico has some BMX features, with a raked top tube, upright handlebars, and thick 20-in wheels that can handle urban pitfalls and potholes. However, the top tube is positioned lower than most city bikes. Its compact mini-bike frame coupled with components has an elongated profile and a high seat to allow riders upright sitting, balance, and better visibility. An integrated 22-in (560-mm) alloy capacious handlebar basket for groceries and similar loads, and another option – a hinge that allows the 15-in (380-mm) frame to be folded in half – make it an ideal vehicle to use for work and play, to carry onto public transportation, or to store in cramped urban settings. A Shimano Altus 8-speed gearset, forged alloy 175 and Steel 44T with chainguard crankset, front and rear aluminum alloy hubs, and double-wall alloy wheel rims with BMX tires and reflectors are some other features. Multiple bright color combinations add to Pico's quixotic appeal.

Puma
Pico

Bianchi
Pista Via Condotti

25–27 lb (11.3–12.24 kg)
💲
bianchiusa.com

Pista Via Condotti, a recent single-speed fixed-gear city/ commuter bike from Bianchi, the legendary Milanese company founded in 1885, bears the firm's hallmark 700c racetrack profile with a short wheelbase for speed, without the price tag of true racing gold-medal-winning versions. Edoardo Bianchi virtually created the racing genre and within a scant three years won an international Grand Prix of Paris, the competition being a forerunner of the Tour de France. His company, now under Cycleurope, is a global brand, the U.S. branch of which is based in California.

This affordable lightweight classic track-bike setup, in a variety of sizes from 49 to 61, has drop handlebars and aluminum components on a signature Celeste blue powder-coated chromoly TIG-welded steel frame and fork; polished chrome parts subtly highlight the design. Top-rate components – Truvativ Touro track chainset/cranks and a 48-tooth chainring, Shimano SS-7600 16-tooth fixed-gear sprockets, Maddux track wheels and skinwalled tires, Velo black cotton tape grips, Velo VL-1156 black suede saddle, and MKS Sylvan pedals – make this a bargain. Brakes and water-bottle clamps are not supplied but can be added.

Umberto Dei
Regale Aurea

$$
$$
33 lb (14.96 kg)
umbertoDei.it; mydutchbike.com

Umberto Dei's eponymous company was founded in 1896 in Italy, and it remains among the country's oldest bicycle producers. Of the many classic city and commuter Umberto Dei bike designs, most have details that have remained unchanged since the 1930s. Umberto Dei's skilled artisans fashion vintage-style bikes by hand, but they are, mechanically speaking, state-of-the-art. The Regale Aurea, inspired by the classic Imperiale and Regale Lusso, has a brazed lugged steel frame, a rear carrier, old-fashioned Chiavelli rod-actuated rim brakes with a front brake modulator, steel cottered chrome-plated cranks, aluminum alloy wheels, a steel chain case, skirt guards for a women's version, leather Dei saddle, tool bag, and hand-sewn handgrips for chromed steel handlebars, bottle generator lights, a ding-dong bell, and a frame-mounted wheel lock. The headlights are lowered to accommodate a front basket, and the fixed-speed bike can be altered with a 3-speed Sturmey-Archer rear hub.

Abici
Serie Stoccolma

27 lb (12.24 kg)
$\bigstrut\bigstrut$
abici-italia.it

Abici, an Italian company formed in 2006 by Giuseppe Marcheselli, Stefano Selletti, and Cristiano Gozzi, goes back to the ABC of urban bicycling, combining traditional 1950s Italian profiles with modern components. The brazed, welded steel frames, with a fully enclosed chainguard, metal mudguards, handcrafted leather saddles, back-pedal rear brakes, manual front brakes, battery lights, and quick-release front wheels even on the simplest versions, are handmade or assembled in Italy, and are usually painted in vintage car colors. Recently, Note Design Studio, the multidisciplinary Swedish product design firm hired to envision Abici's Granturismo line as a new Serie Stoccolma, added shades of white, gold, powder blue, and rust to Abici's already luscious palette, all inspired by iconic Stockholm buildings: Birger Jarls Torg, Sveavägen, Hotorget, and V. Trädgårdsgatan.

Abici
Serie Stoccolma

Biomega
SYD (Sydney)

25–27 lb (11.3–12.24 kg)
$$$–$$$$
biomega.dk

One of Biomega's recent bikes, the SYD (Sydney), was designed by Australian-born furniture and industrial designer Marc Newson, who now works around the world as creative director of Qantas. This model underscores the small quixotic Danish company's global approach to smart-looking green design. A reiteration of an older Newson bike, the innovative lightweight pressure and blow-molded carbon-fiber frame resembles a cyclist in racing mode, adding zip to what is intended as a round-the-town urban bike. The frame can be customized in carbon black, white, or a vibrant, eye-catching, African yellow.

"I approached the bike as an exercise in joining the dots and looked for the simplest form that was able to do this,

to connect the headset to either the bottom bracket or seat and then to the rear wheel," Newson comments. This is also a clever way to invisibly route multiple brake cables. Available with either Shimano 8-speed hubs or as a higher-priced 14-speed model with Rohloff and titanium parts, the SYD is only built to order and is pricey. It's a good thing the frame incorporates a hole to secure it well.

Biomega
SYD (Sydney)

Royal Dutch Gazelle
Toer Populair T3

30 lb (13.6 kg)
$$
gazelle.us.com; mydutchbike.com

Royal Dutch Gazelle bikes are ubiquitous in Amsterdam and other bicycle-mad cities in the Netherlands, the inhabitants of which know this 1892 brand as well as clogs or tulips. Gazelle's classic Toer Populair T3 Omafiets "granny bikes" and Opafiets "gentlemen's bicycles" are still ideal for reliable, 70-degree upright urban commuting. All the traditional practical trappings – fenders, mud flaps, skirt guards, chainguards, rear rack with elastic straps, front Tung Lin wheel dynamo light – remain, complemented by a modern battery-powered rear light, low-maintenance Sturmey-Archer hubs and rod-actuated drum brakes and other components that are guaranteed for ten years.

Gazelle's high-quality parts and steel frames from China are tested and assembled in Holland, and only water-based paints are used to finish the 3-speed bikes. An 8-speed Nexus hub on the T8 version allows more speeds and is better on hills in cities like San Francisco. A Brooks old-style pre-softened B67 saddle, a simple AXA Defender rear wheel lock, and an Original Gazelle Ding-Dong bell add nostalgic touches.

Royal Dutch Gazelle
Toer Populair T3

BMW
Touring Bike

37 lb (16.78 kg)
⇕⇕
shop.bmwgroup.com

More widely known for its motorbikes, the German car company BMW has also been making a range of bikes for 60 years. In 2011, it launched several models that tap into the rising popularity of utility versus sports biking. There is a clean-lined cruise bike in the line, but the more retro, vintage design of the aluminum-frame Touring Bike has more appeal and versatility as a comfortable, albeit heavy, urban bike that can also be used for commuting with a rear rack.

An angled trekking stem allows the height and angle of the saddle to be adjusted as needed; other features include a Suntour NCX-D-LO front suspension fork with 3-in (75-mm) cushioning, and a 24-speed Shimano Alivio derailleur. It is available in four sizes that range from small to extra-large; all are painted a glossy chocolate color with gold accents.

BMW
Touring Bike

Kildemoes
Vintage Singlespeed/ Vintage 321-01

22 lb (9.97 kg)
\$\$
kildemoes.dk

During the 1950s, Børge Kildemoes Cykler grew from Børge Kildemoes' lathe in his farmhouse basement into one of Denmark's largest bicycle companies, now called Kildemoes under the Cycleurope umbrella. Kildemoes' nostalgic, friendly designs range from sports bikes to granny and cruiser profiles, which populate Danish cities in particular but are seen all over Europe. One recent reissue from the archive, the Vintage Singlespeed in reptile green, blue, or brown colors, is eye-catching.

A high-tensile chromoly steel frame with classic round hollow tubing and short sport geometry, strong wheels with built-in double-bottomed aluminum rims, double nipple-reinforced puncture-resistant Spectra Duramax X3 tires,

reinforced stainless-steel spokes, a versatile rear wheel flip-flop hub (fixed-gear wheel on one side and freewheel on the other), horizontal rear dropouts and chain tensioners, and a strong anti-rust chain for the single-speed version make this one of the most elegant urban/touring bikes. The hollow crankshaft with external bearings, aluminum crank arm and steel blade, dual-pivot racer brakes of cold-forged aluminum, a classic racing saddle, and polished aluminum handlebars and seatpost all bring this vintage beauty up to date.

Van Nicholas
Yukon Fixed

18 lb (8.16 kg)
$$$
vannicholas.com

Van Nicholas has produced the Yukon Fixed single-gear racing-style bike for couriers and urban commuters. It is made, like all their bikes, with a titanium frame – each frame hand polished and guaranteed for life. Constructed in a variety of sizes or in bespoke dimensions, the frame is emblazoned with chemically engraved head badges. Lightweight, with slender lines, the slightly flexible shock-absorbing frame tubes are essentially round with tapered chainstays. The slender seatstays taper at the tips. A CNC-machined 2¾-in (68-mm) English threaded bottom bracket, CNC-sculpted titanium dropouts, fender mounts, seatstay, and dropout rack mounts, welded water bottle bosses, and a hand-brushed finish are special features. Continental

Ultra Race tires, Campagnolo Record Triple 170 mm Polish cranksets with Shimano pedals, alloy forks and handlebars, and leather saddle and grips are possible combinations.

Fold-
ing/Inno-
vative

Calfee
Bamboo Bike

18–20 lb (8.16–9.07 kg)
$–$$$
calfeedesign.com

Designer Craig Calfee, from Santa Cruz, California, first used bamboo for a modern bike in 2005 as a publicity gimmick to complement the carbon-fiber frames he has been producing since 1988. "I was intrigued by the ride quality," Calfee says. He thoroughly explored the green medium, which others have only tinkered with. He admired bamboo's tensile steel-like strength and its better-than-concrete compressive qualities. Calfee's bamboo frame geometries are conventional and use commercially produced components, such as Gates Carbon Drive and Rohloff Speedhubs, but his unique mitered joints (guaranteed for ten years) are achieved without metal or carbon, bound only by Chinese hemp soaked in epoxy – like the scaffolding used

for high-rise construction in Asia. "Carbon fiber and bamboo don't get along too well. They are dissimilar. Bamboo shrinks slightly and carbon fiber stays inert," Calfee comments. Now Calfee's stiff, smoke-dried, clear-coated bamboo road and off-road mountain bikes are part of his growing line. Actors Brad Pitt, Angelina Jolie, and Robin Williams, Tour de France winner Greg LeMond, and Ironman winner Dave Scott each ride one. Bamboosero, a low-cost version of the expensive commuter Calfee Bamboo Bike, is being produced in sustainable workshops in Africa.

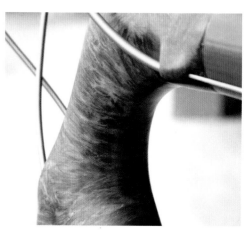

Calfee
Bamboo Bike

Gary Galego
CarbonWood Bike

33 lb (14.96 kg)
$$$$$
garygalego.com

Sydney-based furniture designer Gary Galego introduced a wooden bike at the 2009 annual Milan furniture fair that echoes Copenhagen bicycle designer Jens Martin Skibsted's view that a bike is a kinetic, comfortable piece of furniture. "I put together a show called Workshop to show what's possible," Galego says.

Galego likes wood's aesthetic appeal and its ability to absorb shocks. His laminated birchwood and carbon-fiber sandwich bike frame is as strong as steel and, despite its large sectional volume, the bike and components – Galego's maple, carbon-fiber, and leather handlebar, cranks, and steel forks from Paul's Components in San Diego, and custom wheels – together weigh only about 22 lb (9.97 kg). Carbon

fibers in the front triangle add shear strength and rigidity and, although this makes the frame non-biodegradable, it will last a long time and get passed down. "I hope to make furniture that exemplifies those properties," Galego says. So far, his production time of three to four weeks for one bike keeps the price high.

Gary Galego
CarbonWood Bike

Airnimal
Chameleon

22 lb (9.97 kg)
$$$–$$$$
airnimal.com

Richard Loke's company Airnimal, based in Cambridge, England, has achieved "high performance in a bike that can be folded compactly." However, this is not a typical folding bike but an unusual-looking, high-quality machine that can be dismantled and folded compactly for air travel. The name, derived from its "light-as-air" virtues and the phrase "air transportation," appeals to the designer's sense of fun. Its sporty performance, urban commuter, and rough-road versions are respectively named Chameleon, Joey, and Rhino. The whimsical animal names mask well-tuned frame geometries based on a fat oval tubular aluminum main spar with and without rubber suspension, 20–27 speed Shimano Tiagra groupsets, derailleurs or fixed gears, carbon-fiber

forks, and other quality parts to enhance the light bike's folding functions, rider adjustability, stiffness, and comfort. Buyers can also add mudguards and racks. The Chameleon frame, 20–24-in wheels, handlebar, and seatpost require a little time and patience to dismantle easily, fold, and install in their hard polypropylene travel case or duffle. "There is a strong urban bike movement in the UK. We're interested in the practical side," Loke says. Manufactured in Taiwan and assembled in England since 1999, Airnimal bikes are sold widely around the world, but are best known in the UK.

Airnimal
Chameleon

⊓ucati
Copenhagen Wheel

30 lb (13.6 kg)
$
senseable.mit.edu/copenhagenwheel

Christine Outram and fellow students at MIT's SENSEable City Lab designed a wireless battery and motorized gear system within a red rear wheel bicycle hub that helps cyclists ride over longer distances in flat Copenhagen or to go higher in hilly terrain. Outram and her team's so-called Copenhagen Wheel, unveiled at the 2009 Cop15 United Nations Climate Conference, won a James Dyson design award because it can transform an ordinary bike into an e-bike. It is designed to conquer distance as well as topography in diverse bicycle-friendly cities such as Copenhagen or hilly San Francisco. The battery harnesses and stores energy generated by braking, provides a boost when needed, and simultaneously powers apps that wirelessly gather data such as miles traveled, receive traffic alerts, and even gauge CO_2 levels in the air and cardiac stress. The Wheel, to be produced with Ducati Energia, Italy, is still being refined and, because it uses standard components, it is heavy.

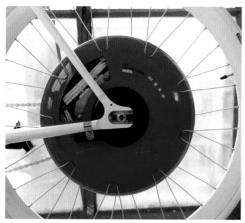

Ducati
Copenhagen Wheel

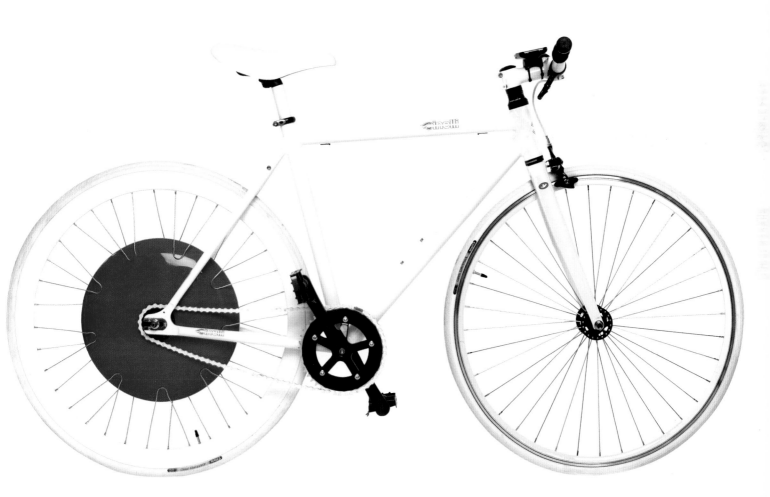

Montague
Crosstown

27 lb (12.24 kg)
$
montaguebikes.com

In Cambridge, Massachusetts, aerospace engineer David Montague heads the eponymous bike company that his father, an overweight architect, founded in 1987 after he designed a sturdy full-size folding bike to keep in his car.

"The original design was simply large and small triangles," Montague explains. By removing the front wheel, the bike became small enough to stash away. A new CLIX single-release mechanism on the top tube is an improvement that has made the original Montague bike foldable and more compact. Rather than breaking the frame, riders can release the lever, fold the frame of 7005 series aircraft-grade aluminum alloy, and stack the easy-to-release front wheel. The Folding Integrated Technology

(F.I.T.) was inspired by the design of full-suspension downhill bike frames.

Montague's new Crosstown model is a practical hybrid commuting bike. It's a 7-speed portable, fast-folding bike with 700c Alex wheels and Kenda Kwick multi-tread tires that ride well over sidewalks and trails. It also features another innovation: an Octagon stem adjuster that allows the handlebars to be raised or lowered to any desired height with the click of a button. A rigid Unicrown fork, SRAM Twist shifters, SRAM X-3 long-cage rear derailleur, and an Alloy brakeset complete the ensemble.

Montague
Crosstown

Puma
Disko

28 lb (12.7 kg)
$-$$ for special editions
puma-bikes.com

German sports shoe-maker Puma first launched its UM (Urban Mobile) bike design in 2005. It was designed by Danish designer Jens Martin Skibsted of Biomega, who has gone on to produce many more bikes for the company. The UM frame evolved into the Puma Bike, the Glow Rider, and more recently the Puma Disko. The limited-edition semi-folding UM bike was the kind of hybrid in which Skibsted specializes. Part-city bike, part-BMX, and part-American cruiser, the European-style UM and its two-toned frame have been reprised in the Puma Disko with 1.95 in-thick tires, shock absorbers for a comfortable ride, a quick-folding top bar design, a 9-speed Shimano SLX transmission for all-terrain riding, V-brakes, folding pedals, and 24-in wheels.

BMX handlebars allow upright riding. The unique down tube, made of ½-in (12-mm) wire cord (like those on Slingshot bikes), can be released, and it doubles as a locking cable. If it is severed, it makes the bike unusable unless a replacement, available only to owners, is supplied.

Puma
Disko

Brompton
Folding Bike

28 lb (12.7 kg)
$$-$$$
brompton.co.uk

The Brompton folding bike for urban or distance commuters was designed and built by engineer Andrew Ritchie in the early 1980s at his home in London. As if to underscore its purpose, the bike continues to be made in a London factory that sits between a railway line and a motorway.

The secret of the bike's success is its sturdy, rigid frame and the ease with which it folds: first back wheel, then front wheels, pedals, and handlebars; the clincher is when the seatpost is released and thrust in to lock the ensemble together into a cube shape. A folded Brompton can be lifted by the saddle into a car trunk, onto a train, or, too big as cabin luggage, checked in on airplanes. Its 1,200 exclusive handmade Brompton parts are supplemented by only a few off-the-shelf components: screws, Sturmey-Archer 3-speed and SRAM 5-speed hubs, and a bicycle chain. Six speeds are achieved with a derailleur. The brazed steel bikes are powder-coated in several colors from shocking pink to simple black or white. Titanium parts help to lower the average 28-lb (12.7-kg) weight of most Brompton models to 20 lb (9.07 kg) for the single-speed, mudguard-less titanium-and-steel S1E-X model.

Brompton
Folding Bike

Bernds
Folding Tandem

36 lb (16.32 kg)
$$$
bernds.de

In 1991, Germans Michaela Buchholz and Thomas Bernds created a well-engineered practical folding bike that could be packed and carried on cycling trips. Now they've applied their folding rear wheel design to a tandem bike. Tandem riders can ride faster more easily with double the power to counter the bike's weight and air-resistance and share a convivial ride in the country. Bernds' light folding tandem makes it eminently transportable to the right location. The hinged folding design of the original Bernds bike remains, as do the Terry Citta foam and gel over stainless-steel frame saddles, 20-in wheels, fat Schwalbe tires, and sprung, folding swing arm. The bike's solid powder-coated frame has been elongated for tandem riding and hinged at the bottom

for ease of the transport; the wheelbase is shortened for stability and for negotiating tight corners in urban traffic. It can carry up to 500 lb (227 kg) of weight. Folded or unfolded, the hinged Bernds tandem with interlocking hinge blades fits in almost all train bike racks and compartments. For transport by car, it can be reduced in size with a few deft moves. A fully adjustable rear handlebar and front rider's saddle, panier racks, and an optional electric drive for hilly terrain make the tandem versatile. Hydraulic brakes allow swift braking even on wet surfaces.

Bernds
Folding Tandem

BSA
Foldman

25 lb (11.3 kg)
⇵
bsahercules.com

Birmingham Small Arms, now more benignly known as BSA, is a brand of TI (Tube Investments) Cycles of India, a part of the Murugappa group in Chennai on the Coromandel coast. Sixty years ago, when the company was founded, cycling was simply a way to get around and was not considered a sporting activity. Now, with its foldable, 20-in wheel Foldman bike, TI/BSA has introduced an affordable, reliable leisure bike for the masses.

The bike's features include soft grips, a polyurethane foam saddle, front and rear alloy V-brakes with long arms for effective braking, 6-speed Shimano thumb gear shifters, straight handlebars for upright riding, and wheel reflectors. Fold-up pedals, a fold-down adjustable handlebar stem, and a hinged steel-alloy frame allow the bike to be folded down into a compact form that can be slipped into a duffle case for storage or transportation in a car trunk.

BSA
Foldman

MIT
GreenWheel G3

18 lb (8.16 kg)
$$
mobile.mit.edu

At the MIT Media Lab in Boston, Massachusetts, Michael Lin, a Master of Science in Architecture and Urbanism, and a leader within the Smart Cities Group run by the late professor William J. Mitchell, explored the viability of electric wheels for bikes.

"I focused on building a robust, long-range wheel and a rear control system," Lin explains.

Lin developed the GreenWheel G3 (akin to the Copenhagen Wheel, see page 156), and exhibited it in Taipei at the biggest international bicycle show. Its simplicity attracted praise and the prospect of mass-production.

The GreenWheel's 250W 7-lb (3.17-kg) motor, lithium-ion battery pack, and patented power-output mechanism hide within an aluminum hub with a rotating outer hub casing attached to the wheel rim. "It all depends on the battery inside. We don't want users to mess with that," Lin says. The battery provides invisible torque going uphill and more power for up to 22 miles (35 km) when cycling on flat terrain. The encased mechanism has an external controller to recharge the battery, adjust the power output, or read the remaining battery level. It even troubleshoots. The internal computer could monitor mileage, user patterns, and CO_2 levels in the environment, and transmit such data to designated cell phones. Early GreenWheel adopters can buy one for the price of an electric bike. Shown here is the GreenWheel on a Montague bike.

Ralf Kittmann
HMK 561 Motorbike

35 lb (15.87 kg)
$$$$
ralf-kittmann.de

Ralf Kittmann, a young industrial designer based in Berlin, has created a motorbike frame that is so light and slender it may well be adapted for a pedal-assisted e-bike.

Seeking a new paradigm for eco-conscious two-wheelers, Kittmann consulted engineers at the Institute for Aircraft Design in Stuttgart to design a frame that could be quickly braided together with unbroken carbon fibers over a mold using a textile-weaving machine. His lightweight electric bike concept, named HMK 561 (for Heizen mit Kohle, or "Heating with Coal/Carbon"), won an IF award, in part because of this new molding technique but also because it deploys the continuous carbon fibers to conduct power to the motorbike's electronic equipment. Similarly, the front and rear suspension stems swinging from the frame conduct power to the bike's two contra-rotating electric propulsion motors, located neatly between the unusual double rims of each wheel.

The one-piece carbon frame serves as an electricity conduit for the tachometer and lighting, and also stores unused power generated by braking in its carbon "circuits." The nearly weightless carbon bike with its lithium polymer battery would reduce energy consumption because "It transports the weight of a person and not the machine," Kittman explains.

Pacific Cycles
IF (Integrate Folding) Mode bike

33 lb (14.96 kg)
$$$
pacific-cycles.com

If the folding STRiDA was British inventor Mark Sanders' "Little Engine That Could," his new award-winning IF (Integrated Folding) Mode, developed with Pacific Cycles, may be its hard-working, grown-up cousin. Ryan Carroll and Michael Lin, who helped Sanders on the design, aimed the IF at commuters who need a greasefree, foldable, full-size bike that rolls and fits anywhere. The aluminum-alloy monocoque-frame IF-Mode bike has 26-in wheels, and its technology is different from that of Sanders' mini-bike. A simple hinge and a snap-in lock on the top bar are used to fold and unfold this new 2-speeder. Magnets in the wheels snap its folded halves together, the pedals fold down, and the Velo VL-2064 brown saddle and Promax SP-728 seatpost can be pushed in to make the bike more compact to wheel along. The chain is hidden in sealed housing, disc brakes are at the centers of both wheels, and tapping a pin in the pedal crank activates the gearshift between the pedals. Kenda Kwick Roller Sport 26 x 1.5-in tires handle potholes well, and the bike carries riders up to 185 lb (83.91 kg) in weight.

Pacific Cycles
IF (Integrate Folding)
Mode bike

Boardman Bikes
IU (Intelligent Urban) concept

boardmanbikes.com

Former Olympic cyclist Chris Boardman, now a prominent sports commentator, has proposed a concept bike that is as beautiful as it is action-packed. His one-piece carbon-fiber and toughened-resin frame vision has a built-in anti-theft lock activated by the bike owner's fingerprints. LED lights embedded in the headset and rear frame double as brake lights, all powered by micro-dot solar cells on the frame and wheel surfaces. A lithium polymer storage battery can be recharged through a USB port for software upgrades. Handlebars are home to GPS displays and sound and speed controls, while the shock-absorbent, pivoting seat arm and saddle are adjustable. An automatic gear-changing shaft drive is concealed inside the frame to the rear rim. Thin tire rings rotate outside the fixed rims on low-friction bearings, and the pneumatic tires contain a self-healing liquid to fix punctures. Luggage can be stashed into the rear wheel cavity, keeping the weight lower to the ground. All the technologies are already here, and the bicycle "could be built now," Boardman claims; "it's just that nobody's put them all together before."

Boardman Bikes
IU (Intelligent Urban)
concept

GP Design Partners
JANO dual bike

38 lb (17.23 kg)
$$$
gp.co.at

European bike designers are exploring renewable materials because they perform better than metals or carbon fiber. The Jano, a tested laminated wood prototype by designer Roland Kaufmann, was created for Vienna's GP Design Partners. Its form, inspired by the pliant material rather than straight tubular steel, resembles a friendly moped or bentwood skis.

"Wood is abundant in Europe. It absorbs shocks and noise like carbon fiber yet has the responsiveness of steel," says Kaufmann. "Wood can be laterally stiff but it has tension and torsion. To keep it light, we use lamination."

The Jano's tactile surface is enhanced by a soft-touch finish and user-friendly technology: a compact gearshift hub, rear-wheel suspension combined with a greaseless toothed belt-drive in a maintenance-free hub, and integrated LED lights and reflectors powered by a low-resistance hub dynamo. A rechargeable battery/motor in the frame's cavity could transform it into a pedelec. Unlike mountain, racing, trekking, or even city bikes designed for specific purposes, the hybrid Jano is meant for leisure rides and distance commuting. Saddlebag and luggage carriers provide cargo options, and the bike's steeply angled steerer and 26-in wheels work well on curves and bends. The anticipated cost is as much as a good racing bike.

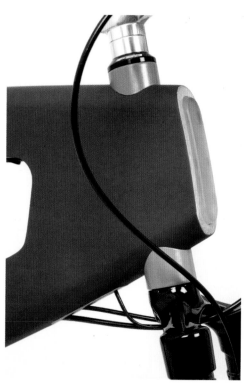

GP Design Partners
JANO dual bike

Velorbis
Leikier

36 lb (16.32 kg)
$$$
velorbis.com

The relatively new Danish bike manufacturer Velorbis has revived pre-war classic Dutch-style bikes made in Germany and distributes them from Copenhagen. However, Leikier, their 2009 limited-edition custom-order powder-coated reinforced steel design with a chopper-style steel fork by blacksmith/designer Lars Leikier, is entirely made in Denmark. Inspired by 1950s motorcycles, the unisex A-frame design includes unusual arrow-shaped stainless-steel handlebars, an alloy chainguard, a Sturmey-Archer front dynamo 5-speed hub and drum brakes, and rear Shimano Nexus 7-speed hub and coaster brake, alloy anti-slip pedals, Van Schothorst stainless-steel rims, no-maintenance stainless-steel spokes and fasteners,

Schwalbe Fat Frank cream tires, reflectors on the tire side walls, pedals, rear and head Busch & Müller lamps, an integrated AXA MTB click 3 lock in silver, a double stand, a classic ding-dong bell, Brooks leather B67 saddles, grips, and mud flaps.

Velorbis
Leikier

BMW
Mini Folding Bike

25 lb (11.3 kg)
⇕
mini.de/shop

Munich's BMW Group car brands include the Mini, and the company now offers a bike to match that folds down small enough to fit into the smallest of cars. Intended as a hedge against city-center traffic, the bike is commute-worthy and ideal for public transportation; its unique folding mechanism allows it to be folded and unfolded in seconds along the crossbar and handlebars. Its comfortable Selle Royal gel saddle can also be retracted, and the reflective pedals fold up. Its lightweight fused-aluminum frame has a Dahon Slipstream, aluminum U7 double-butt fork, 20-in Schwalbe tires on Kinetix Comp rims, and a mat-black double-butt aluminum handlebar. Front and rear mudguards, Kinetix V-front and rear brakes, Avid FR-5 shifters, and wheel reflectors are standard for all-weather riding. The fully assembled mat-black 8-speed bike has silver accents with a Teflon-coated greaseless neon yellow Taya Octo bike chain and yellow bell, and still "flies" the old standard: a Union Jack decal adorns the rear forks.

BMW
Mini Folding Bike

Moulton
New Series Double Pylon

25 lb (11.3 kg)
$$$$$
moultonbicycles.co.uk

The New Series Double Pylon Moulton bike, a descendant of engineer Alex Moulton's iconic 1962 small-wheeled F-frame full-sized original, has a beautiful, skeletal edge-brazed tubular stainless-steel pylon frame engineered for lightness, strength, and speed. Like other Moulton spaceframe bikes, it breaks from big-wheel diamond-frame bike convention by dispensing with a top bar and instead uses two separable pylons held together by a removable head pin. Its hydrolastic, rubber-cone front and rear suspension system was invented by Moulton (a scion of rubber magnate Spencer Moulton) for the BMC Mini car nearly half a century ago. The toy-like, high-pressure tires reduce drag, but without suspension they would be too bumpy

to ride. Perfectly engineered for comfort, Moultons have earned respect and awards, especially after winning the world speed record for a bike ridden in an upright position. Handcrafted in Bradford on Avon, England, where Moulton first started, the Double Pylon has a Brooks Swift saddle, a Moulton Wishbone handlebar, Campagnolo Super Record 2x11 transmission with a Moulton 10-28 stem, Reynolds heat-treated steel fork with stainless-steel dropouts, 20-in Moulton M406 rims with stainless-steel spokes, and optional fenders and luggage carrier.

Moulton
New Series Double Pylon

Tjeerd Veenhoven
Ordinary Carbon Bike

18 lb (8.16 kg)
$
tjeerdveenhoven.com

Dutch industrial designer Tjeerd Veenhoven's lightweight carbon-fiber bike is a startlingly simple concept bike that resembles a spontaneous pencil sketch. His Ordinary Carbon Bike, created for Connecting Concepts, a traveling design show, uses epoxy resin-dipped carbon fibers that are stretched between recycled bike components mounted in a jig (like many lines connecting dots) and allowed to harden. Low-cost, do-it-yourself, and inexpensive, the Carbon Bike can be quickly produced without molds. The resulting bike is rigid and easy to control, although, because it lacks flexibility, "it is not comfortable to use on bumpy surfaces," the designer admits. A seat softer than the Brooks leather saddle shown might solve that problem.

"The essence of my design is to use the material's properties simply. Carbon fibers can be used for a new chair as easily as they can be made into a lightweight bike by anyone," says Veenhoven. A bike that gets you to and from work can even be viewed as an office chair, he suggests.

When his affordable Carbon Bike gets developed for urban use, it will be engineered to carry more weight and to be more shock-absorbent.

Tjeerd Veenhoven
Ordinary Carbon Bike

Bernds
PackBernds

45 lb (20.41 kg)
$$$
bernds.de

In 1991, Germans Michaela Buchholz and Thomas Bernds created a well-engineered practical folding bike that could be packed and carried on cycling trips. Now the designers have applied their award-winning folding rear wheel design to a cargo bike. The Bernds cargo bike is based on their low step-through Gretel frames. The small 20-in Schwalbe wheels and the low-slung powder-coated frame design keep the standard wooden cargo box low and close to the center of the bike. Weights close to 500 lb (227 kg) can be carried with ease in the lightweight basket, which is larger than what most cargo bikes offer. For folding, rear-swing arms with self-lubricating sintered brass bushing and optional fold or push-fit pedals are supplied. As always, the

Bernds bikes use standard seatposts and stems so they can be adapted for individual idiosyncrasies. A standard rear-wheel elastomer suspension with a choice of three degrees of hardness, along with optional front-wheel suspension forks, ensure comfort. A standard V-brake, optional hydraulic wheel brake, or disc brake is provided. A Terry Citta foam and gel over steel frame saddle, an aluminum U-profile 36-spoke wheel rim, and Moon handlebars come as standard.

Bernds
PackBernds

Grace
Pro E-bike

70 lb (31.7 kg)
$$$–$$$$
grace.de

Another example of Germany's burgeoning interest in pedelecs and e-bikes, the snappy Grace e-bike by Michael Hecken and Karl-Heinz Nicolai is produced in Berlin.

Grace's CNC powder-coated aluminum frame has a familiar yet tough-looking diamond profile. This energy-saving eco-conscious roadrunner reaches 22 mph (35 kmh) for up to 12–30 miles (19–48 km) on its fully charged bank of 70 lithium-ion batteries, even in hilly cities. A few solar panels can recharge the battery pack in an hour. It slides discreetly into the frame and powers a self-maintaining 1300W brushless motor encased in the water-resistant back wheel. The batteries also power lights, a horn, and a computer panel on the handlebar that shows bike speed, battery level,

and wattage consumed per second. Powerful headlights, legally required for e-motorbikes, appear on Grace frames configured for racing, commuting, or touring, with SRAM gears and Magura 204-mm disc brakes and pedals. The Grace Pro city bike is a luxury made-to-order vehicle for upright riding. A less expensive Grace One version will soon be available with fewer custom options. With a specially developed fork, a slightly smaller and lighter engine, forged aluminum parts, and one standard color, it will cost about half the price of Grace Pro.

Grace
Pro E-bike

Biomega
Rio Bamboo Bike

25–32 lb (11.3–14.5 kg)
$$$$
biomega.dk

British furniture and product designer Ross Lovegrove deployed bamboo for Rio, a high-end "stronger-than-steel" bike frame that he designed for Danish design firm Biomega. "We were the first to view the bicycle as a lush piece of design – furniture for locomotion," says Biomega founder Jens Martin Skibsted. Flavio Deslandes, a bamboo expert in Brazil, cultivates the hard, fast-growing "parts" that are later assembled in Copenhagen. Transporting materials is never carbon-neutral, but Lovegrove's design, unveiled in Taiwan and Milan in the same month, "is a metaphor for change" from a car culture to a greener bike world, the designer claims. Others have made bamboo bikes, but Lovegrove's sleek version uses innovative clamps to grip the bamboo frame. An aluminum stem adds strength, while an integrated shaft drive keeps grease off clothing. A 20-in diamond frame, 26-in tires with reflective strips, an 8-speed Shimano rear hub and roller brake, as well as a front disc brake, complete the bike.

Bleijh Concept & Design and Design Amsterdam
Sandwich Bike

sandwichbikes.com

A concept bike of reinforced plywood takes bike design into IKEA terrain, with a flat-pack system that could conceivably be assembled by anyone who can accurately read an exploded diagram. In bike-happy Amsterdam, interdisciplinary designer Basten Leijh of Bleijh Concept & Design, and illustrator Pieter Janssen of Design Amsterdam, wished for a bike made of well-engineered quality components that most people could afford, and gravitated toward a concept that brings labor costs down. Their concept brings a new perspective to bike design, production, and distribution that could do a lot toward promoting an eco-conscious transportation future. Two wooden or composite material computer-cut pallets make up the frame of the bike, which is assembled with a single tool and held together simply by four identical "smart cylinders" that house the cranks, axle, head tube, and seatpost. The flat sandwich sides provide surfaces – not unlike sandwich advertising placards – for personalized branding. It may not be the fastest or lightest bike, but at the right price, fleets of such Sandwiches could be assembled for free use in cities choked by car traffic.

The Shadow E-Bike, perhaps the first wireless bike, is produced by Toronto-based Daymak, an electric novelty bike import company launched in 2001 by Yeg Baiocchi.

The bright yellow Shadow – Daymak's first serious venture into transportation vehicles – is the result of six tested prototypes. Lacking cable brakes and gears, it has an easy-release front wheel that contains the bike's crucial technology: a 250W or 350W electric motor, a 36V 10AH lithium-ion battery, USB and charging ports, wireless transceivers (on an aluminum disc that does not spin), an LED battery power display, and braking technology. Perry Coaster rear brakes are coupled with a magnetic regenerative front brake that helps to recharge the battery, which lasts about 12–15 miles (19–24 km) on a single charge. Wireless pedal-assist stretches that to 20 miles (32 km). The battery takes four to five hours to recharge, so monitoring it via wireless ISM 2.4 GHz frequency-hopping spread-spectrum technology becomes important. A wireless speed throttle and a monitoring panel are attached to the handlebars. The full-suspension, powder-coated Y-shaped aluminum alloy frame looks toy-like, yet absorbs 23 mph (38 kmh) speeds, and the bike's 26-in spokeless wheels have tough weather- and impact-resistant polyurethane hubcaps.

Daymak
Shadow E-Bike

Silverback Technologies
Starke 1

31 lbs (14 kg)
₴₴₴
silverbacklab.com

Dynamo-powered lighting for bikes is not new, but German company Silverback Technologies may have the distinction of being the first to supply a front wheel hub that converts wheel rotation into electricity for USB sockets to charge a GPS or iPod. The USB port atop the handlebars of their 2012 one-size-fits-all flow-formed nickel alloy Starke 1 city bike is a standard feature. Riders can power their gadgets at a speed of 7 to 9 mph (11–15 kph) and keep LED lights on for up to five minutes after pedaling stops. Starke 1 also has a separate 100w motor hidden in its seat bag that can be activated when pedaling uphill with the push of a button.

SBC Starke alloy forks, Alex SX44 rims, a Supernova Infinity S Dynamo in the front and Shimano Deore LX hub in the rear, Schwalbe Marathon Supreme 26-in tires, Shimano XT 9-speed shifters and rear derailleur, Shimano Alfine 2 piece crankset and bottom bracket, a Shimano 9 speed 11-32T cassette, VP components pedals, and hydraulic Shimano disc brakes are other features in its mountain bike-like profile.

Silverback Technologies
Starke 1

STRiDA
STRiDA 5

19 lb (8.61 kg)
$
strida.com

In 1985, Royal College of Art student Mark Sanders worked on a commuter bike that he could fold and roll to class like a folded baby buggy. His triangular-frame design, called STRiDA, was original; it became the first mass-produced foldable bicycle, winning its greatest fans in Asia, particularly Japan. The 22-lb (9.97-kg) tubular 7000-aluminum alloy and plastic invention (like a bulky walking stick on wheels when folded) snapped open into a bike within seconds. Over time, improvements have made it tilt-proof and even lighter, but strong enough to carry a 250-lb (113-kg) rider. A Kevlar belt instead of a standard chain, fast-stopping discs in lieu of drum brakes, a welded bottom bracket, and 16-in aluminum-alloy rim wheels with black skin-wall tires with reflective Scotchlite strips and aluminum hubs instead of nylon and plastic made the single-speed STRiDA 5 even stronger and lighter. The fenders are rubber/plastic, and the optional luggage rack carries up to 30 lb (13.6 kg). The STRiDA LT retains all-weather fiberglass and nylon wheels.

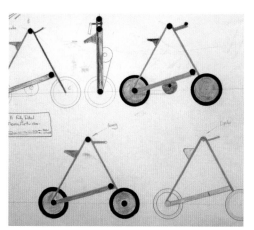

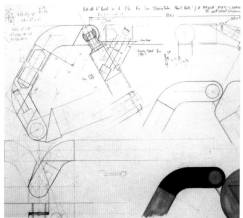

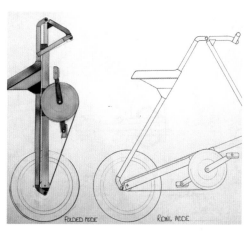

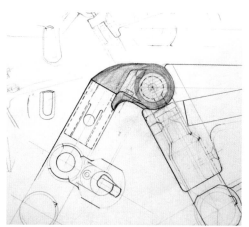

STRiDA
STRiDA 5

TreeHugger
ThinBike

25 lb (11.3 kg)
$$$
schindelhauerbikes.com

Graham Hill, founder of the green design blog TreeHugger.com, collaborated with Schindelhauer Bikes to adapt their city bike design for Hill's tiny city apartment in New York, where storage space is minimal. Hill wanted a full-size bike with foldable pedals and a swiveling, foldable handlebar that could be stored flush against a hallway wall. The result, Hill's so-called ThinBike, became an online favorite, not so much because it is an original idea (Airnimal and other folding bikes achieve thinness), but because it uses standard components that could retrofit any bike: a Speedlifter rotating stem and MKS folding pedals turn the bike into a slimmer custom package.

ThinBike has a standard diamond 6061 aluminum-alloy, TIG-welded, triple-butted hand-assembled Schindelhauer frame with a cut rear triangle with a locking system for a carbon belt drive. Standard features include the silent, greaseless Gates Carbon Drive belt, a leather Brooks saddle, an 11-speed Shimano Alfine hub, Rapidfire shifters, Schindelhauer Ergo antique brown hand pedal leather grips, an integrated Tange Seiki headset, tough Continental City Ride tires with reflex stripes, quick-release catches, Alexrims G6000, Hollowtech crankset, Tektro-forged aluminum dual-pivot brakes, an integrated Kalloy seatpost, and aluminum forks.

TreeHugger
ThinBike

CycleEco
Vienna Bike

37 lbs (16.7 kg)
$$
valentinvodev.com

A production-ready pedelec, the aluminum Vienna Bike by Red Dot design award-winner Valentin Vodev is actually a trike that has an F-frame with back wheels placed close together. Uniquely, they have no shared axle and are connected by separate arms to the frame. Rubber suspension (like in a Mini car) enables each wheel to go up or down, left or right independently, and turns corners smoothly just like a bike. "That's the innovation here," Vodev says.

A pin below the uncommon suspension and near the cranks can be unlocked for the bike to pivot and fold. "Pedaling, steering, suspension, and folding all happen there," Vodev says.

The chain and gears are in one back wheel arm and the battery and motor in the other. At a pedaling speed of about 3 mph (5 kph), a computerized panel indicates the moment to turn the motor on. The motor stops automatically when the trike hits 10 mph (16 kph) – faster than most cars in city traffic. A fully-charged battery lasts for about 25 miles (40 km).

A wheeled polypropylene storage pod that snaps onto the back rack has an extendable handle to allow it to be pulled along by hand when shopping. Developed with grants from the Austrian government and advice from London-based creative director Sebastian Conran, Vienna may soon appear in at least two European capitals.

CycleEco
Vienna Bike

Hyuk-Jae Chang
Ville concept

whoisjae.com

In response to the growing numbers of bike riders in U.S. cities, Hyuk-Jae Chang, a Korean industrial designer based in Pittsburgh, Pennsylvania, embarked on Ville, a street bike proposal for Cannondale that can be used for urban transportation as well as a shopping cart. A wooden mockup was first tested and then rendered as a finished product in CAD to demonstrate the merits of the easy-to-fold design.

According to Chang, urban cyclists have disincentives to use a bike when they have to carry packages or go shopping because of a lack of places to park a bike securely or to protect it from vandalism or theft. In response to that problem, Chang's Ville bike concept doubles as a shopping cart or trolley when it is partially folded. A small third wheel folds out to stabilize the cart. Ville can also be folded more compactly for storage or transportation. "This allows the bike to remain with the user indoors and out," says Chang; "Ville answers the needs of users who desire environmentally friendly transportation, but have been discouraged due to the limitations of normal bicycle designs."

STRiDA, Brompton, and Moulton folding bikes were all sources of inspiration; however, Chang wanted Ville "to be more useful than just transportation."

Dahon
Vitesse D7

26 lb (11.79 kg)
$$
dahon.com

Dr. Alex Moulton, inventor of hydrolastic suspension for the Mini, pioneered folding bikes in England in 1962. Twenty years later, another aeronautical scientist, Dr. David Hon at Hughes Aircraft Corporation in California, became his American counterpart. Dr. Hon's Dahon Folder design was immediately admired for its portability. Thanks to venture capital and a factory in Taiwan, the first mass-produced Dahons emerged in 1983. Dr. Hon's simpler, lighter, faster, and stronger folding bikes incorporated innovations such as quick-release latches, vector frames, hydroformed frames, auto locks, luggage sockets, V-clamps, and lockjaw hinges.

Dahon bikes, now produced in China and Bulgaria, include affordable 7-speed Vitesse D7s that take 15 seconds to fold to less than half their open size. Easy to carry on public transportation, the Vitesse, available in many colors, is an effective, if not fast, urban vehicle. Its features include Radius V telescope handleposts, adjustable V-clamps, 6061-T6 aluminum flat handlebars, BioLogic ergonomic grips, a BioLogic Como or Selle Royale Alpine Gel saddle, Suntour folding pedals, 20-in Dahon Rotolo or Schwalbe Citizen tires, a Dupont L3 lubricated shift cable, ProMax V aluminum linear spring brakes, and SRAM shifters. The 7005 butted aluminum alloy Sonus tube frame has a Lattice Forged hinge and an integrated fork that can handle tall, 230-lb (104-kg) riders.

Stevens
Carpo White Pedelec

42 lb (19.05 kg)
$$$
stevensbikes.de

Few companies win accolades as often as Stevens, based in Hamburg, Germany. A wholesaler of premium bike components, Stevens began to produce carbon-and-steel mountain, trekking and race frames during the 1990s. A recent IF award for Stevens' Ventoux carbon road frame and praise for its light Vuelta alloy frame vindicate the brand's popularity.

Now that Stevens [see pages 56 and 46] has a stylish e-bike with an auxiliary motor in its repertoire, it may help to tip the balance in favor of bikes in hilly cities. The pedal electric cycle, or pedelec, has a small 250W Bosch engine with a 36V lithium-ion battery neatly attached to the 7005TB aluminum frame to give riders a continuous variable boost when climbing hills or going distances of 25–50 miles (40–80 km). The motor, 26-in wheels, and a NuVinci N360 drivetrain can boost speeds up to 15 mph (25 kmh). The bike's other features include hydraulic Shimano disc brakes, FSA Metropolis crankset, Oxygen City Grip pedals, Oxygen Scorpo wheel rims, Super Moto 26-in tires, and a Selle Royal Viper saddle with a manganese frame. A Bosch 1500 computer with a display screen, controls three ride modes: eco, sport, and speed. Oxygen Scorpo Riser aluminum handlebars permit upright riding.

Access-
ories

Pricing key:
Under $100: $
Under $200: $$
Under $300: $$$
Under $500: $$$$

Brompton
A Bag
$$$$
brompton.co.uk

Faris Elmasu
Bent Basket
$$
bentbasket.com

A stylish Spanish leather attaché-style bicycle messenger bag by British folding bike company Brompton is fine enough for the boardroom. A Bag's internal dividers for files, folders, or a laptop are set off by an attractive felt lining that also appears on the bag's padded shoulder strap. A bright-colored rainproof cover is visible even in driving rain. Hanging frames and carriers cost extra.

Faris Elmasu, a young industrial designer based in San Francisco, first thought of making a simple Eamesian bentwood bike carrier that dispenses with ungainly bungee cords when he was still a student traversing Parisian back streets on a bike. His elegant patent-pending traylike Bent Basket is made of vacuum-formed laminated white oak (or walnut) veneer and wide elastic nylon straps that are slipped into keyhole slots cut into the molded wood form. Four criss-crossed straps can quickly hold down a 12-pack of beer and a sweater or a bag of groceries with ease. The unique basket is bolted to a special aluminum armature and wheel stays. It can be detached to use as a carrier basket too.

Copenhagen Parts
Bike Porter
$$
3.6 lb (1.63 kg)
copenhagenparts.com

Knife & Saw
Bike Shelf
$$$
theknifeandsaw.com; missionbicycle.com

The Bike Porter, designed by Goodmorning Technology for Copenhagen Parts, a Danish manufacturer of unusual bicycle parts, is a novel lightweight aluminum-alloy basket integrated with bike handlebars. It can hold up to 33 lb (14.96 kg) of goods. The sturdy carrier-cum-basket breaks new ground for modern urban bikes and is theftproof. It can be installed like regular handlebars using a two-part head stem.

Artist and graphic designer Christopher Brigham created this elegant, low-tech, all-in-one wood shelf and bike hanger in a woodshop owned by a Google engineer and his wife in San Francisco. Brigham's company Knife & Saw now produces the popular Bike Shelf elsewhere in the United States, where ash and walnut wood are abundant. Securely fixed to the wall with a mounting cleat and screws, the Bike Shelf can conveniently hold books, flowers, a helmet, or keys; to hang a bike, simply slide its top bar into an angled cleat-like slot cut into the boxy shelf's face.

Basil
Birke Wire Basket
$
basil.nl

Basil
Brava II Fine Mesh Pannier
$
evanscycles.com

The spacious Birke front grocery and carrier basket of fuchsia-colored coated steel wire by Dutch company Basil is designed to be used with BasEasy system holders (not included). A black plastic grip makes it easy to hold the pannier.

The ovoid Brava II front basket is just one of many options offered by Basil, a Dutch company that specializes in panniers made of traditional wicker and extra-fine wire mesh, like this one with a reinforced bottom. This design may not be compatible with all bikes. A BasEasy mount (which costs extra) makes it simple to take the basket off, and a wide foam-insulated handle makes it easier to carry.

Design House Stockholm
Carrie Basket
$
designhousestockholm.com

Andrew Lang
Cycloc Bicycle Wall Mount
$
cycloc.com

From Design House Stockholm, Carrie, a tough, weatherproof, molded polypropylene bicycle pannier with metal mounts by Swedish designer Marie-Louise Gustafsson, looks as fragile as a crocheted lace tablecloth. Easy to unmount, the filigreed Carrie basket has an optional polyester carrying strap for shopping or picnic excursions. Upturned, it can even serve as a "covered" picnic table.

Cycloc, a cylindrical hanger to store bikes on walls, is the brainchild of British designer Andrew Lang. A mounting panel is bolted or screwed securely to a wall as needed to store the bike horizontally or vertically. Cycloc's slotted cylindrical shape of new or postindustrial recycled molded plastic is designed to grip top tubes snugly and to hold bikes away from the wall; a bike's weight wedges it into Cycloc's slots more tightly. Gloves and scarves can be stored inside the cylindrical hanger, and a standard U-shaped bike lock can be slipped through holes in the cylinder to secure the bike. Cycloc is available in orange, green, black, and white.

The capacious 24-liter Folding Basket, a simple nylon fabric pannier by British bike company Brompton, is like a large file folder with an open top. It is extremely convenient for carrying groceries and light goods. The box-shaped basket has a hinged bracing frame that allows it to be folded flat for storage. Drainage holes provide easy drainage in case the inside gets wet.

Folding Crate by San Francisco's Public is as simple, practical, and affordable as it looks. It is essentially a collapsible plastic storage box that can be attached to any rack with ties slipped through custom-drilled holes in the bottom of the box. When not in use, the crate can be detached, folded, and stored.

Retrovelo
Frame Bag
$$$$
retrovelo.de

Quarterre
Hood
$$$$
quarterre.com

Bicyclists with a penchant for classic frames with straight top tubes and no back or front racks can opt for German company Retrovelo's thick leather Frame Bag, which echoes those used by the Swiss military a century ago. Separate compartments within these classic, elegantly detailed attaché-style bags for carrying laptops, notebooks, or lunch are modern updates. Frame bags can be thrown over a top tube like saddlebags and quickly fastened to the seat tube with two belt hooks and a Tenax button.

Daniele Ceccomori, Clive Hartley, Nick Mannion, and Jason Povlotsky of Quarterre, a versatile industrial design firm based in London, England, have created a set of witty, artful bike furniture that is beautifully made. Hood, their least expensive piece, is a white powder-coated steel hood that looks like origami. The front lip is folded back to form a wide invisible hook to store a city bike by its top bar. The hook is lined with a strip of leather to protect the bike's finish. The top of the Hood forms a helmet shelf, while the bottom tip folds up to form a small hook for gloves or other paraphernalia. An inner bracket with holes allows for a bike lock to be slipped through.

Velorbis
Old School Leather Satchel
$$$$
velorbis.com; mydutchbike.com

Rickshaw
Pipsqueak Handlebar Bag
$
rickshawbags.com

Like school bags of yore, Copenhagen's Velorbis bike satchel is made of sturdy calfskin leather with a large front pocket, three internal compartments, and one zippered pocket in the rear. Styled to fit into office settings as well, it looks like a briefcase that can be used to transport laptops. A long adjustable/detachable leather shoulder strap adds to the satchel's usability and portability.

Mark Dwight, who made Timbuk2, the Prada of bike messenger bags, also founded Rickshaw bags, a relatively new San Francisco manufacturer of colorful messenger and bike bags that can be customized and ordered online. The tiny, lightweight Cordura nylon Pipsqueak bag, with waterproof lining and Velcro straps, attaches easily to handlebars or belts. It is large enough to store wallets, keys, phones, and even dog treats.

MIO
Pop-Up Bicycle Basket
$
mioculture.com

Clarijs
Saddlebags
$$
mydutchbike.com; workcycles.com

Philadelphia-based designers Isaac and Jaime Salm started their company making 3D wall coverings of recycled paper before coming up with another eco-conscious product: a flat-pack laser-cut powder-coated recycled steel pannier that can be assembled by the user. Designed in conjunction with Brian Kelly, the one-piece Pop-Up Bicycle Basket can be mounted in the front or rear section of a bike with supplied stays and attachments.

Colorful saddlebags handmade in many sizes by Clarijs in the Netherlands are more than just fashion statements. They are sturdy, simple workhorses for carrying groceries, the makings of a picnic lunch, laptops, and office supplies. Tough, waterproof, cadmium-free bisonyl fabric for truck tarps has been deployed to make these hardy carriers with quick-release buckles and reflective tapes on both sides. The bags' Velcro loops attach easily to most rear racks.

Basil's Select-Double dark gray double saddlebag is made of water-repellent nylon. Its zippered interior and exterior pockets, elastic bottle bands, and reflectors for cycling after dark make it a practical, versatile choice for storage on the move.

The STRiDA Triangle Bag, although intended to fit snugly within foldable STRiDA bike frames (see page 194), can be used on other bikes too. Designed by STRiDA creator Mark Sanders in England and produced by American manufacturer Areaware, the leather and weatherproof nylon bag is large enough to carry tools, cell phones, or headphones.

Twin Panniers by San Francisco's Public were clearly inspired by traditional European bicycle bags or saddlebags that attach to rear racks on most bicycles. Equipped with carrying handles, Public's version can be taken inside easily when the bike is parked. Large enough to hold a lock, helmet, or jacket, the waterproof bags are also strong enough to hold groceries and heavy laptops. Made of durable white trucking tarp fabric with colorful top flaps, easy-release buckles, and reflective tapes for nighttime safety, the relatively affordable bag also has a steel grommet for securing it to a rear rack.

Made of Danish ash wood and stainless steel screws, Velorbis wood crates – branded with the company's rampant lion crest – are vintage-looking to suit the company's retro-style bikes. Sturdy enough to carry bottles, groceries, or gym bags, the boxes are like the classic fruit crates seen in Holland or Denmark for nearly a century. The boxes fit onto front carriers and can be harnessed to them using metal hooks. They are available in large or small sizes, with or without lids.

Web Resources

Abici
abici-italia.it

Airnimal
airnimal.com

All Modern
allmodern.com

Andrew Lang
cycloc.com

Armitage Bike Shop
armitagebikeshop.com

Audi
audi-collection.com/Cycling

Basil
basil.nl

Bella Ciao
bellaciao.de

Bernds
bernds.de

Bianchi
bianchi.com

BIG (Bjarke Ingels Group)
big.dk

Bike Arch
bikearc.com

Bikestation
bikestation.com

Biomega
biomega.dk

Bleijh Concept & Design
sandwichbikes.com

BMW
shop.bmwgroup.com
mini.de/shop

Boardman Bikes
boardmanbikes.com

Breezer
breezerbikes.com

Brompton
brompton.co.uk

BSA
bsahercules.com

Calfee
calfeedesign.com

Christophe Machet
cristophemachet.com

Cicli Pinarello
pinarello.com

Cinelli
cinelli.it

Colnago
colnago.com

Copenhagen Parts
copenhagenparts.com

Crescent
crescent.se

Cube
cube.eu

CycleEco
valentinvodev.com

Dahon
dahon.com

Dario Pegoretti
Pegoretticicli.com

Daymak
daymak.com

Design House Stokholm
designhousestockholm.com

Ducati
senseable.mit.edu/
    copenhagenwheel

ECAL
ecal.ch

Elian Cycles
eliancycles.com

Evans Cycles
evanscycles.com

Faris Elmasu
bentbasket.com

Ferrari
store.ferrari.com

Focus
focus-bikes.com

Frost Produkt
altabikes.no

Fuji
fujibike.com

Gary Galego
garygalego.com

Giant Bicycles
michael-young.com
giant-bicycles.com

GP Design Partners
gp.co.at

Grace
grace.de

Haro
harobikes.com

Hyuk-Jae Chang
whoisjae.com

Ibis
ibiscycles.com

Joey Ruiter
jruiter.com

Kestrel
kestrelbicycles.com

KGP Design Studio
kgpds.com

KiBiSi
kibisi.com

Kildemoes
kildemoes.dk

Knife and Saw
theknifeandsaw.com

Koga
koga.com

Lapierre
lapierre-bikes.co.uk

Mac Bike
macbike.nl

Manifesto Architecture
mfarch.com

Marcos Madia
coroflot.com/mmadia

Mercedes-Benz
mercedes-benz-access-
ories.com

Mio
mioculture.com

Mission Bicycle
missionbicycle.com

MIT
mobile.mit.edu

Montague
montaguebikes.com

Monty
monty.es

Moulton
moultonbicycles.co.uk

MyDutchBike
mydutchbike.com

NeilPryde
neilprydebikes.com

Orbea
orbea.com

Pacific Cycles
pacific-cycles.com

Porsche
porsche-bike.com

Public
publicbikes.com

Puch
puch-fietsen.nl

Puma
puma-bikes.com

Quarterre
quarterre.com

Ralf Kittman
ralf-kittmann.de

Retrovelo
retrovelo.de

Rickshaw
rickshawbags.com

Royal Dutch Gazelle
gazelle.us.com

Schindelhauer Bikes
schindelhauerbikes.com

SE
sebikes.com

Seven
sevencycles.com

Silverback Technologies
silverbacklab.com

Slingshot
slingshotbikes.com

Sögreni
sogrenibikes.com

Specialized
specialized.com

Stevens
stevensbikes.de

STRiDA
strida.com

Surly
surlybikes.com

Tjeerd Veenhoven
tjeerdveenhoven.com

Trek
trekbikes.com

Umberto Dei
umbertodei.it

Urban Arrow
urbanarrow.com

Vanmoof
vanmoof.com

Van Nicholas
vannicholas.com

Vanilla
vanillabicycles.com

Velorbis
velorbis.com

WorkCycles
workcycles.com

Credits

Acknowledgments

Many serendipitous events and connections have led to this book. I'll start with thanks to my blue 1980s era Motobecane Super Mirage 12-speed bike that launched my bicycling career in San Francisco and to my friend and publisher Laurence King who instigated this book in London decades later.

In 2009, an encounter in Copenhagen with urban bike designer Jens Martin Skibsted at a dinner party in his home during the Index design award festivities made me aware of his colleagues Lars Larsen and architect Bjarke Ingels and others who passionately promote technologically and visually sophisticated bikes as a way to green urban realms. Among such people, are bamboo and carbon fiber frame designer Craig Calfee in Santa Cruz, USA, who was introduced to me by his former mentor Sam Cuddeback. Also in the United States, Rob Forbes, founder of Design Within Reach, whose new-found passion for Public bikes has infected San Francisco, New York and points between, as well as Palo Alto architect Jo Bellomo whose chic bike storage arcs on the west coast and in Hawaii (which I have written about in the San Francisco Chronicle presciently anticipated a greater interest in urban biking. Bicycles, an off-site exhibition from the Oakland Museum of California shed much light on the Bay Area's role in the growth of mountain biking. Photographer James Newman, a former bike messenger who has documented many bikes for Public, introduced me to the world of "fixies" and single-speed bikes. New Yorker Graham Hill's Treehugger.com site was an invaluable touchstone for my most eco-conscious choices and Britons Mark Sanders, inventor of the STRiDA, and sportsman Chris Boardman eloquently highlighted how folding and sports frame technologies have enhanced other contemporary bikes. The nearly simultaneous launch of great hybrid city bikes by design-savvy car manufacturers Porsche, Audi, BMW, Mercedes Benz and Ferrari added greatly to my conviction that, especially in dense city centers, bikes will be the preferred vehicles of the future.

That future seems to be here. My great thanks to the city of Amsterdam for convincing proof of this one early morning when I spent a few hours on a canal-side bench watching hundreds of people on black granny bikes on their way to work or giving their preschoolers, strapped into panniers, a ride to school. Ecological, healthful and practical notions aside, special thanks go to Lilian Tilmans who later guided me across Amsterdam's picturesque northern dikes on a beefy red Batavus MacBike for the first time: it was pure fun.

My thanks also go to all the individual photographers and companies that have contributed images for this book, and to my meticulous editor, Donald Dinwiddie.